The Quest for

MEEKNESS
and
QUIETNESS of SPIRIT

MATTHEW HENRY

The
Quest
for

MEEKNESS and QUIETNESS of SPIRIT

WIPF & STOCK · Eugene, Oregon

Wipf and Stock Publishers
199 W 8th Ave, Suite 3
Eugene, OR 97401

The Quest for Meeknes and Quietness of Spirit
By Henry, Matthew
ISBN 13: 978-1-55635-769-5
ISBN 10: 1-55635-769-9
Publication date 12/10/2007
Previously published by Wm. B. Eerdmans, 1955

Contents

To the Reader:

I do not think it at all needful to tell the world what it was which led me to the writing of this discourse concerning Meekness, the substance of which was preached many years ago; nor am I concerned to apologize for the publication of it: if I thought it needed an apology I would not consent to it. That temper of mind which it endeavors to promote, and charm men into, everyone will own to be highly conducive to the comfort of human life, the honor of our holy religion, and the welfare and happiness of all societies, civil and sacred: and therefore, while the design cannot be disliked, I hope what is weak and defective in the management, will be excused. Some useful discourses have been of late published against rash anger, and an excellent dissuasive from revenge by the present Bishop of Chester; wherein those brutish vices are justly exposed. I am cooperating in the design, while I recommend the contrary virtues to the love and practice of all that profess relation to the Holy Jesus. And if this essay have that good effect upon those into whose hands it shall at any time fall, my object will be attained.

Matthew Henry

Chester, Nov. 21, 1698

Introduction

*Even the ornament of a meek and quiet
spirit, which is in the sight of God of great
price.*   1 PETER 3:4

THE apostle Peter in this Epistle (as also his beloved
brother Paul in many of his) is very emphatic in pressing upon Christians the conscientious discharge of the duties of
their particular relations, and not without good reason. For
generally it holds true that we are really as we are relatively.
He is here in the former part of this chapter directing Christian wives how to conduct themselves in that relationship,
to the glory of God, their own comfort, and the spiritual benefit and advantage of their husbands. And among other good
lessons he teaches them how to dress themselves as is becoming to women professing godliness. Those of that sex are
commonly observed to be very solicitous about their ornaments. When the question is asked, Can a maid forget her ornaments, or a bride her attire? it is supposed scarce possible
(Jer. 2:32). This prevailing inclination the Apostle here
takes hold of, so as to recommend those graces and duties
which are indeed the most excellent for the amiable adorn-
ment not only of the sex to whom the exhortation is primarily
directed, but of the other also for whom no doubt it is likewise intended. Observe the Apostle's method:

1. *He endeavors to wean them from the vanity of outward ornaments* (vs. 3) "whose adorning let it not be that
outward adorning . . ." This does not forbid the sober and
moderate use of decent ornaments, when the use is according
to the quality, place, and station, and in due season (not on

days of fasting and humiliation, when it is proper for ornaments to be laid aside (Ex. 33:4-5). But it forbids the inordinate love and excessive use (that is, the abuse) of them.
There may be the plaiting of the hair, and the wearing of
gold, and there must be the putting on of apparel. That
shame which came into the world with sin has made it
necessary. But we must not make these things our adorning; that is, we must not set our hearts upon them, nor value
ourselves by them, nor think the better of ourselves for them,
nor pride ourselves in them, as if they added any real excellence to us. Nor are we to say to them as Saul did to
Samuel, honor me now before this people. For he did it of
a vain ambition to make a fair show in the flesh. We must
spend no more care, or thoughts, or time, or words, or cost
about them, and lay no more stress or weight upon them
than they deserve, and that is but a very little. It is but
glory hung upon us, as the expression is (Isa. 22:24), and
has no glory if compared with the glory that excells it even
in the creatures that are far below us. For Solomon in all
his glory was not arrayed or beautified like one of those lilies
which today is, and tomorrow is cast into the oven. We must
not seek these things first, nor seek them most, as if we had
bodies for no other end but to bear our clothes, and had
nothing else to do with them but to make them fine. It was
the folly, and proved the ruin of that rich man in the parable
that he made his purple and his fine linen (with other ornaments and delights of the body), his good things, the
things in which he placed his happiness, and in which
he had his consolation (Luke 16:19, 25). That is, in the
language of this scripture, he made them "his adorning"
(2 Cor. 3); and so, being unclothed of these, he was found
naked. Let not the wearing of gold, and the putting on of
apparel be *kosmos* — "the world," so it may be rendered:
it is *mundus muliebris* — "a woman's world." Let not these

things be all the world with us, as they are with many, who reckon that to be out of the fashion (whatever it be) is to be out of the world (Gal. 1:4; 1 John 4). Christians are called out of the world, and delivered from it, and should evidence a victory obtained by faith over it. As in other instances, so in this. It is a prescribed rule of our holy religion (whether they will hear, or whether they will forbear), that "women adorn themselves in modest apparel, with shamefacedness and sobriety" (1 Tim. 2:9). But whereas there are some, on the one hand, that exclaim against vanity in apparel as the crying sin of this age above any other, as if it were a new thing under the sun, and as though the former days were in this respect better than these (Eccl. 7:10); and whereas others on the other hand condemn it as a piece of fanaticism to witness (as there is occasion) against this vanity — both may receive a sufficient answer if they but read that excellent homily of the Church of England entitled, *An Homily against Excess of Apparel,* by which it will appear that even in those early days of the Reformation it was a vanity that prevailed much in our land, and which the rulers of the church thought themselves obliged to reprove. But we will hasten to the text.

2. *He endeavors to bring them in love with the better ornaments,* those of the mind, the graces of the blessed Spirit, here called "the hidden man of the heart." Grotius observes that "though he writes to women, yet he uses a word of the masculine gender, because the ornament he recommends is such as both men and women must be adorned with." Grace, as a living principle of regular holy thoughts, words, and actions, is sometimes called the "new man" (Eph. 4:24), sometimes the "inward man" (Rom. 7:22; 2 Cor. 4:16), and so here, the "hidden man of the heart." It is called a man, because it is made up of many parts and members, and its operations are vital and rational;

and it restores those to the dignity of men who, by sin, had made themselves like the beasts that perish.

It is called the "man of the heart" because out of the heart are the issues of life; there lie the springs of the words and actions, and therefore into that the salt of grace is cast, and so all the waters are healed (2 Kings 2:21). He is the Christian indeed, that is one inwardly, and that circumcision, that baptism, which is "of the heart" (Rom. 22:29). It is called the "hidden man of the heart" because of the work of grace is a secret thing, and does not make a pompous show in the eye of the world. It is a "mystery of godliness" (Col. 3:3); a life that is hid with Christ in God to whom secret things belong. Therefore the saints are called his hidden ones (Ps. 83:3) for the world knows them not, much less does it yet appear what they shall be. The king's daughter that is espoused to Christ is "all glorious within" (Ps. 45:13). The working of grace in the soul is often represented as a regeneration, or being begotten again; and perhaps when this good work is called the "hidden man of the heart" (Ps. 139:14-16) there may be some allusion to the forming of the bones in the womb of her that is with child, which Solomon speaks of as unaccountable, as is also the way of the Spirit (Eccl. 11:5; John 3:8). And lastly, it consists in that which is not corruptible. It is not depraved or vitiated by the corruption that is in the world through lust, and is in the soul a "well of living water, springing up unto eternal life" (John 4:14).

In the text he specifies one particular grace, one member of this hidden man of the heart, which we must every one of us adorn ourselves with, and that is "a meek and quiet spirit which is in the sight of God of great price." Two things may be observed.

(1) *The grace itself here recommended to us:* It is a "meek and quiet spirit." There must be not only a meek and quiet

behavior outwardly; there may be that, either by constraint, or with some base and disguised design, while the soul in the meantime is rough and turbulent and envenomed; the words may be softer than oil, while war is in the heart (Ps. 55:21). But the word of God is a discerner and judge of the thoughts and intents of the heart (Heb. 4:12). The power of men's laws may bind a man to good behavior, but it is only the power of God's grace that will "renew a right spirit" within him (Ps. 51:10). It is this that makes the tree good, and then the fruit will be good. The God with whom we have to do demands the heart, looks at the principle, and requires truth in the inward parts, not only in the duties of his own immediate worship, that those be done in the Spirit, but also in the duty we owe to our neighbor, that that also be done with a pure heart and without dissimulation. The word of command which the Captain of our salvation gives is, Christians, take heed to your spirits (Mal. 2:15).

(2) *The excellency of this grace*: It is "in the sight of God of great price." It is really a precious grace, for it is so in the sight of God, and we know that he can neither deceive, nor be deceived. It is the same word that is used in 1 Tim. 2:9 for that costly array, which is joined with gold and pearls. Persons of quality, in their ornaments, affect not so much that which is gay, as that which is rich; not that which makes a glittering, gaudy show, and pleases children and fools, but that which is of intrinsic value, and recommends itself to the intelligent. A meek and quiet spirit is such an ornament, which has not that gaiety which is agreeable to the humor of a carnal world, but that real worth which recommends it to the favor of God. It is one of those graces which are compared to the "powders of the merchant" (Song of Solomon 3:6), far-fetched, and dear-bought, even with the precious blood of the Lord Jesus. Herein we should every one labor and this we should be ambitious of, as of the greatest honor,

that present or absent, living and dying, we may be "accepted of the Lord"; and blessed be God it is a thing attainable, through the Mediator from whom we have received instruction how to walk so as to please him. We must walk with meekness and quietness of spirit, for this is "in the sight of God of great price." Therefore this mark of honor is, in a special measure, put upon the grace of meekness, because it is commonly despised and looked upon with contempt by the children of this world as a piece of mean-spiritedness. But (however they be termed and treated now) they are happy, and will appear so shortly, whom God approves, and to whom he says, "Well done, good and faithful servant"; for by his judgment we must stand or fall eternally.

These words, therefore will easily afford us this plain doctrine: that meekness and quietness of spirit is a very excellent grace which we should every one of us put on and be adorned with.

In the prosecution hereof, we shall endeavor to show: *First*, what this meekness and quietness of spirit is; *Second*, what excellency there is in it, and, *Third*, how to apply it.

The Nature of Meekness
and Quietness of Spirit

1

The Nature of Meekness
and Quietness of Spirit

MEEKNESS and quietness seem to import much the same thing, but the latter having something of metaphor in it, will illustrate the former, and therefore we shall speak of them distinctly.

I. *We must be of a meek spirit.*

The critics translate the word *facilis* as *easy*. Meekness is easiness of spirit; not a sinful easiness to be debauched, as Ephraim's, who willingly walked after the commandment of the idolatrous princes (Hos. 5:11), nor a simple easiness to be imposed upon and deceived, as Rehoboam's who when he was forty years old is said to be young and tender-hearted (2 Chron. 13:7), but a gracious easiness to be wrought upon by that which is good, as theirs whose heart of stone is taken away and to whom a "heart of flesh" is given. Meekness is easiness for it accomodates the soul to every occurrence, and so makes a man easy to himself and to all about him. The Latins call a meek man *mansuetus* (*manu assuetus* — used to the hand), which alludes to the taming and reclaiming of creatures wild by nature and bringing them to be tractable and familiar (James 3:7,8). Man's corrupt nature has made him like "the wild ass used to the wilderness, or the swift dromedary traversing her ways (Jer. 2:23, 24), but the grace of meekness, when that gets dominion in the soul, alters the temper of it, brings it to hand, submits it to management; and now the wolf dwells with the lamb and the leopard lies down with the kid, and a little child may lead them; for enemies are laid aside, and there is nothing to "hurt or destroy" (Isa. 11:6,9).

Meekness may be considered with respect both to God and to our brethren. It belongs to both the tables of the law and attends upon the first great commandment, "Thou shalt love the Lord thy God"; as well as the second, which is like unto it, "Thou shalt love thy neighbor as thyself"; though its special reference is to the latter.

1. *There is meekness toward God,* and it is the easy and quiet submission of the soul to his whole will, according as he is pleased to make it known whether by his word or by his providence.

a. *It is the silent submission of the soul to the word of God:* the understanding bowed to every divine truth, and the will to every divine precept; and both without murmuring or disputing. The word is then an engrafted word when it is received with meekness (James 1:21), that is, with a sincere willingness to be taught and a desire to learn. Meekness is a grace that cleaves the stock, and holds it open, that the word, as the imp or shoot, may be grafted in; it breaks up the fallow ground and makes it fit to receive the seed; it captivates the high thoughts and lays the soul like white paper under God's pen. When the dayspring takes hold of the ends of the earth, it is said to be turned as clay to the seal (Job 38:12-14). Meekness does, in like manner, dispose the soul to admit the rays of divine light which before it rebelled against; it opens the heart as Lydia's was opened; it sets us down with Mary at the feet of Christ, in 'the place and posture of the learner (Deut. 33:3). The promise of teaching is made to the meek because they are disposed to learn: "The meek will he teach his way" (Ps. 25:8,9). The word of God is gospel indeed, good tidings to the meek (Isa. 61:1), they will entertain it and bid it welcome; the poor in spirit are evangelized (Matt. 11:5) and wisdom's alms are given to those that with meekness "wait daily at her gates," and like beggars "wait at the posts of her door" (Prov. 7:34). The language of this meekness is that of the child Samuel, "Speak, Lord, for thy servant heareth" (1 Sam. 3:9), and that of Joshua who, when he was in that high post of honor, giving command to Israel, and bidding defiance to all their enemies (his breast filled with great and bold thoughts), yet upon the intimation of a message from heaven thus submits himself to it: "What saith my Lord unto his servant?" (Josh. 5:14). And that of Paul (and it was the first breath of a new man), "Lord, what wilt thou have me to do?" (Acts 9:6). And that of Cornelius, "And now we are all here present before God, to hear all things that are commanded thee of God" (Acts 10:33). And that of the good man I have read of who, when he was going to hear the word used to say, "Now let the word of the Lord come; and if I had six hundred necks, I would bow them all to the authority of it." To receive the word with meekness is to be delivered into it as into a mold: it seems to be Paul's metaphor (Rom. 6:17), that form of doctrine "into which you were given up." Meekness softens the wax, that it may receive the impression of the seal, whether it be "for doctrine or reproof, for correction or instruction in righteousness." It opens the ear to discipline, silences objections, and suppresses the risings of the carnal mind against the word, consenting to the law that it is good and esteeming "all the precepts" concerning all things to be "right" even when they give the greatest check to flesh and blood.

b. *It is the silent submission of the soul to the "providence" of God concerning us.*

(1) *When the events of providence are grievous and afflictive,* displeasing to sense, and crossing our secular interests,

meekness not only quiets us under them but reconciles us to them, and enables us not only to bear but to receive evil as well as good at the hand of the Lord, which is the excellent frame that Job argues himself into (Job 11:10). It is to kiss the rod, and even to accept of the punishment of our iniquity, taking all in good part that God does, not daring to strive with our Maker, no, nor desiring to prescribe to him, but dumb and not opening the mouth because God does it. How meek was Aaron under the severe dispensation which took away his sons with a particular mark of divine wrath! "He held his peace" (Lev. 10:3). God was sanctified, and therefore Aaron was satisfied, and had not a word to say against it. Unlike to this was the temper, or rather the distemper, of David who was not like a man after God's own heart when he was "displeased because the Lord had made a breech upon Uzziah" (2 Sam: 6:8), as if God must have asked David leave thus to assert the honor of his ark. When God's anger is kindled ours must be stifled; such is the law of meekness that whatsoever pleases God must not displease us. David was in a better frame of mind when he penned the 56th psalm, the title of which, some think, bespeaks the calmness and submissiveness of his spirit when the Philistines took him in Gath. It is upon Jonath-elem-reckokim, "the silent dove afar off." It was his calamity that he was afar off, but he was then as a "silent dove," mourning perhaps (Isa. 38:14), but not murmuring, not struggling, not resisting when seized by the birds of prey; and the Psalm he penned in this frame was *Michtam*, a "Golden Psalm." The language of this meekness is that of Eli, "It is the Lord" (1 Sam. 3:18), and that of David to the same purport, "Here I am, let him do to me as seemeth good unto him" (2 Sam. 15:26). Not only he *can* do what he will, subscribing to his power, for who can stay his hand? Or, he *may* do what he will, subscribing to his sovereignty, for he gives not account

of any of his matters. Or, he *will* do what he will, subscribing to his unchangeableness, for he is in one mind, and who
can turn him? But, "Let him do what he will," subscribing
to his wisdom and goodness, as Hezekiah said, "Good is the
word of the Lord" (Isa. 39:8). Let him do what he will, for
he will do what is best; and therefore if God should refer
the matter to me, says the meek and quiet soul, being well assured that he knows what is good for me better than I do for
myself, I would refer it to him again. He shall "choose our
inheritance for us" (Psalm 47:4).

(2) *When the methods of providence are dark and
intricate* and we are quite at a loss what God is about to
do with us, "his way is in the sea, and his path in the great
waters, and his footsteps are not known," clouds and darkness are round about him, a meek and quiet spirit acquiesces
in an assurance that all things shall work together for good
to us if we love God, though we cannot apprehend how or
which way. It teaches us to follow God with an implicit
faith, as Abraham did when he went out not knowing very
well whom he followed (Heb. 11:8). It quiets us with this,
that though what he doeth "we know not now," yet we
"shall know hereafter" (John 13:7). When poor Job was
brought to that dismal plunge that he could no way trace the
footsteps of the divine providence, but was almost lost in that
labyrinth, how quietly does he sit down with this thought,
"But he knows the way I take; when he hath tried me, I
shall come forth as gold" (Job 23:8, 9).

2. *There is meekness toward our brethren,* toward all
men (Tit. 3:2), and so we take it here. Meekness is especially conversant about the affection of anger, not wholly
to extirpate and eradicate it out of the soul (that were to
quench a coal which sometimes there is occasion for, even
at God's altar, and to blunt the edge even of our spiritual
weapons, with which we are to carry on our spiritual war-

fare), but its office is to direct and govern this affection that we may "be angry and not sin" (Eph. 4:26).

Meekness, in the school of the philosophers, is a virtue consisting in a mean between the extremes of rash excessive anger on the one hand, and a defect of anger on the other, in which Aristotle confesses it very hard exactly to determine.

Meekness, in the school of Christ, is one of the "fruits of the Spirit" (Gal. 5:22, 23). It is a grace (both *gratis data,* "freely given," and *gratum faciens,* "rendering kind"), wrought by the Holy Ghost both as a sanctifier and as a comforter in the hearts of all true believers, teaching and enabling them at all times to keep their passions under the conduct and government of religion and right reason. I observe that it is wrought in the hearts of all true believers because though there are some rough and knotty pieces that the Spirit works upon, whose natural temper is unhappily sour and harsh, which are long in the squaring; yet wheresoever there is true grace, there is a disposition to strive against, and strength in some measure to conquer, that distemper. And though in this, as in other graces, an absolute sinless perfection cannot be expected in this present state, yet we are to labor after it, and press towards it.

More particularly, the work and office of meekness is to enable us prudently to govern our own anger when at any time we are provoked, and patiently to bear out the anger of others that it may not be a provocation to us. The former is its office especially in superiors, the latter in inferiors, and both in equals.

a. *Meekness teaches us prudently to govern our own anger* whenever any thing occurs that is provoking. As it is the work of temperance to moderate our natural appetites toward those things that are pleasing to sense, so it is the work of meekness to moderate our natural passions

against those things that are displeasing to sense, and to
guide and govern our resentments of those things. Anger
in the soul is like mettle in a horse, good if it be well managed. Now meekness is the bridle, as wisdom is the hand
that gives law to it, puts it into the right way and keeps it in
an even, steady, and regular pace in that way, reducing it
when it turns aside, preserving it in a due decorum, and re-
straining it and giving it check when at any time it grows
head-strong and outrageous and threatens mischief to ourselves and others. It must thus be held in, "like the horse
and mule, with bit and bridle" (Psalm 32:9), lest it break
the hedge, run over those that stand in its way, or throw
the rider himself headlong. It is true of anger, as it is true
of fire, that it is a "good servant," but a "bad master"; it is
good on the earth, but bad in the hangings. Now meekness
keeps it in its place, sets banks to this sea, and says, "Hitherto thou shalt come, and no further; here shall thy proud
waves be stayed."

In reference to our own anger, when at any time we meet
with the excitement of it, the work of meekness is to do
four things:

(1) *To consider the circumstances* of that which we
apprehend to be a provocation, so as at no time to express
our displeasure, but upon due and mature deliberation. The
office of meekness is to keep reason upon the throne in the
soul as it ought to be, to preserve the understanding clear
and unclouded, the judgment untainted and unbiased in
the midst of the greatest provocations, so as to be able to set
everything in its true light and to see it in its own color, and
to determine accordingly, as also to keep silence in the court
that the still small voice in which the Lord is (as he was with
Elijah at Mount Horeb, 1 Kings 19:12, 13) may not be
drowned by the noise of the tumult of the passions. A meek
man will never be angry at a child, at a servant, at a friend

till he has first seriously weighed the cause in just and even balances, while a steady and impartial hand holds the, scales, and a free and unprejudiced thought judges it necessary. It is said of our Lord Jesus that "he troubled himself" (John 11:33), which denotes it to be a considerate act and what he saw reason for. Then things go right in the soul when no resentments are admitted into the affections, but what have first undergone the scrutiny of the understanding, and thence received their pass. That passion which comes not in by this door but climbs up some other way is a thief and a robber, against which we should stand upon our guard. In a time of war (and such a time it is in every sanctified soul in a constant war between grace and corruption) due care must be taken to examine all passengers, especially those that come armed, whence they come, whither they go, whom they are for, and what they would have. Thus should it be in the well-governed, well-disciplined soul. Let meekness stand sentinel, and upon the advance of a provocation let us examine who it is that we are about to be angry with, and for what. What are the merits of the cause, wherein lay the offence, and what was the nature and tendency of it? What are likely to be the consequences of our resentments, and what harm will it be if we stifle them, and let them go no further? Such as these are the interrogatories which meekness would put to the soul, and in answer to them would abstract all that which passion is apt to suggest and hear reason only, as it becomes rational creatures to do.

Three great dictates of meekness we find put together in one scripture: "Be swift to hear, slow to speak, slow to wrath" (James 1:19). Some have observed that these three dictates of meekness are expressed in three proper names of Ishmael's sons: Mishma, Dumah, Massa (Gen. 25:14). Bishop Prideaux in the beginning of the wars recommended to a gentleman who had been his pupil these three words as the summary of his advice: Mishma Dumah, Massa; the signification of which is: "Hear, Keep silence, Bear." Hear reason, keep passion silent, and then you will not find it difficult to bear the provocation.

It is said of the Holy One of Israel when the Egyptians provoked him, *Libravit semitam irae suae* — "He weighed a path to his anger," as the margin reads it from the Hebrew (Psalm 78:50). Justice first poised the cause, and then anger poured out the vials. In Genesis 11:5 the Lord came down to see the pride of the Babel-builders before he scattered them, and in Genesis 18:21 he came down to see the wickedness of Sodom before he overthrew it, though both were obvious and barefaced. This he did to teach us to consider before we are angry, and to judge before we pass sentence that herein we may be "followers of God, as dear children," and be merciful, as our Father which is in heaven is merciful.

We read of the "meekness of wisdom" (James 3:13); for where there is not wisdom (that wisdom which is profitable to direct, that wisdom of the prudent which is to understand his way), meekness will not long be preserved (Eccl. 10:10, Prov. 14:8). It is our rashness and inconsideration that betray us to all the mischiefs of an ungoverned passion, on the neck of which the reins are laid (which should be kept in the hand of reason), and so we are hurried upon a thousand precipices. Nehemiah is a remarkable instance of prudence presiding in just resentments. He says, "I was very angry when I heard their cry" (Neh. 5:6, 7), but that anger did not at all transgress the laws of meekness, for he continues, "Then I consulted with myself," or as the Hebrew has it, "My heart consulted in me." Before he expressed his displeasure, he retired into his own bosom, took time for a sober thought upon the case, and then he "rebuked the nobles" in a very solid, rational discourse (Neh. 5:8-11) and the success was good (Neh. 5:12, 13). In every cause, when passion demands immediate judgment, meekness moves for further time and will have the matter fairly argued, and counsel heard on both sides.

When the injured Levite had pitched upon a very barbarous course to irritate the tribes of Israel (who commonly were too fiery to need a spur) against the men of Gibeah, yet withal he referred the matter to their deliberate counsels, to teach us when our hearts are meditating revenge to do likewise (Judg. 19:30). So and so the matter is, "consider of it, take advice," and then "speak your minds." When Job had any quarrel with his servants he was willing to admit a rational debate of the matter and to hear what they had to say for themselves. "For what shall I do when God riseth up?" he says. And withal, "did not he that made me in the womb, make him?" (Job 31:13-15). When our hearts are at any time hot within us we should do well to put that question to ourselves which God put to Cain, "Why am I wroth?" (Gen. 14:6). Why am I angry at all? Why so soon angry? Why so very angry? Why so far transported and dispossessed of myself by my anger? What reason is there for all this? "Do I well to be angry for a gourd that came up in a night, and perished in a night?" (Jonah 4:6). Should I be touched to the quick by such a sudden and transient provocation? Will not my cooler thoughts correct these hasty resentments, and therefore were it not better to check them now? Such are the reasonings of the meekness of wisdom.

(2) *The work of meekness* is to calm the spirit so that the inward peace may not be disturbed by any outward provocation. No doubt a man may express his displeasure against the miscarriages of another, as much as at any time there is occasion for, without suffering his resentments to

recoil upon himself and to put his own soul into a hurry. What need is there for a man "to tear himself (his soul, so it is in the Hebrew) in his anger?" (Job 14:4). Cannot we charge home upon our enemy's camp without the wilful disordering of our own troops? Doubtless we may, if meekness have the command, for that is the grace which preserves a man master of himself, while he contends to be master of another, and which, though there may be some firing in the outworks, yet fortifies the heart, the main fort, the inner wards, against the assaults of provocation, which do us no great harm, while they do not rob us of our peace, nor disturb the rest of our souls. As patience in case of sorrow, so meekness in case of anger, keeps *possession* of the soul (as the expression is in Luke 21:19), that we be not dispossessed of that freehold, and takes care when the bell is up, that it does not overturn. The drift of Christ's farewell sermon to his disciples we have in the first words of it: "Let not your hearts be troubled" (John 14:1). It is the duty and interest of all good people, whatever happens, to keep trouble from their hearts, and to have them even and sedate, though the *eye* (as Job expresses it) should continue unavoidable in the provocation of this world (Job 17:2). The wicked (the *turbulent* and *unquiet* as the word primarily signifies) are "like the troubled sea when it cannot rest" (Isa. 57:20), but that peace of God, which passeth all understanding, keeps the hearts and minds of all the meek of the earth. Meekness preserves the mind from being ruffled and discomposed, and the spirit from being unhinged by the vanities and vexations of this lower world. It stills the noise of the sea, the noise of her waves, and the tumult of the soul; it permits not the passions to crowd out in a disorderly manner, like a confused, ungoverned rabble, but draws them out like the trained bands, rank and file, every

one in his own order, ready to march, to charge, to fire, to
retreat, as wisdom and grace give the word of command.

It is said of the just and holy God that he is "Lord of
his anger." The translation "He is furious" (Nah. 1:2) is
perhaps not so well, for "fury is not in him" (Isa. 27:4),
but he is "The Lord of anger, *compos irae,*" as some of the
critics render it. He is master of his own anger, and we
should labor to be so too. Some interpreters give this as the
sense of that which God said to Cain, "Unto thee," or "subject unto thee, shall be its desire, and thou shalt rule over
it" (Gen. 4:7); that is, over this passion of anger, which
thou hast conceived in thy bosom, thou shouldst, and (if
thou wouldst use the grace offered to thee) thou mightst
subdue and keep under these intemperate heats, so that they
may not disquiet the repose of thy soul, nor break out into
any extravagance.

(3) *Meekness will curb the tongue* and keep the mouth
as with a bridle when the heart is hot (Psalm 39: 1, 2, 3).
Even then, when there may be occasion for a keenness of
expression, and we are called to *rebuke sharply* (cuttingly,
Tit. 1:13), yet meekness forbids all fury and indecency of
language, and everything that sounds like "clamor and evil-
speaking" (Eph. 4:31). The meekness of Moses was not at
hand when he spoke that unadvised word, *rebels* (Num.
22:10); for which he was shut out of Canaan, though
rebels they were, and at that time very provoking. Men in
passion are apt to give reviling language, to call names, and
those most senseless and ridiculous, to take the blessed name
of God in vain, and so to profane it. It is a wretched way by
which the children of hell vent their passion at their beasts,
their servants, any person, or any thing, that provokes them,
to swear at them. Men in a passion are apt to reveal secrets,
to make rash vows and resolutions which afterward prove a
snare, and sometimes to slander and belie their brethren,

and bring railing accusations, and so to do the devil's work; and to speak that in their haste concerning others (as David in Psalm 116:11 said, "All men are liars"), which they see cause to repent of at leisure. How brutishly did Saul in his passion call his own son, the heir-apparent to the crown, the "son of the perverse rebellious woman" (1 Sam. 22:30), that is, "the son of a strumpet," a fine credit to himself and his family. *Racca* and *Thou fool* are specified by our Savior as breaches of the law of the sixth commandment (Matt. 5:22), and the passion in the heart is so far from excusing such opprobrious speeches (for which purpose it is commonly alleged), that really it is that which gives them their malignity, they are the smoke from that fire, the gall and wormwood springing from that root of bitterness; and if "for every idle word" that men speak (Matt. 12:36), much more for such wicked words as these must they give an account at the day of judgment. And as it is a reflection upon God to kill, so it is to curse men that are made after the image of God (though ever so much our inferiors), that is, to speak ill of them, or to wish ill to them.

This is the disease which meekness prevents, and is "in the tongue a law of kindness" (Prov. 31:26). It is to the tongue as the helm is to the ship (it is the apostle's comparison, James 3:4), not to silence it, but to guide it, to steer it wisely, especially when the wind is high. If at any time we have conceived passion, and thought evil, meekness will "lay the hand upon the mouth" (as the wise man's advice is, Prov. 30:32) to keep that evil thought from venting itself in any evil word, reflecting upon God or our brother. It will reason a disputed point without noise, give a reproof without a-reproach, convincing a man of his folly without calling him a fool, will teach superiors either to "forbear threatening" (Eph. 61:9) or (as the margin reads it) to *moderate* it, and will look *diligently*, lest "any root of bitter-

ness, springing up, trouble us, and thereby we" and many
others "be defiled" (Heb. 12:15).

(4) *Meekness will cool the heat of passion* quickly, and
not suffer it to continue. As it keeps us from being soon
angry, so it teaches us, when we are angry, to be soon pacified. The anger of a meek man is like fire struck out of
steel, hard to be got out, but when it is out, soon gone. The
wisdom that is from above, as it is gentle, and so not apt to
provoke, so it is "easy to be entreated" when any provocation
is given (James 3:17) and has the ear always open to the
first proposals and overtures of satisfaction, submission, and
reconciliation, and so the anger is turned away. He that is
of a meek spirit will be forward to forgive injuries, and to
put up with affronts, and has some excuse or other ready
wherewith to extenuate and qualify the provocation which
an angry man (for the exasperating and justifying of his
own resentments) will industriously aggravate. It is but
saying, "There is no great harm done, or, if there be, there
was none intended, and peradventure it was an oversight,"
and so the offence being looked at through that end of the
perspective which diminishes, it is easily past by, and the
distemper being taken in time, goes off quickly, the fire is
quenched before it gets head, and by a speedy interposal the
plague is stayed. While the world is so full of the sparks of
provocation, and there is so much tinder in the hearts of
the best, no marvel if anger comes sometimes into the
bosom of a wise man, but it rests only in the "bosom of
fools" (Eccl. 7:9). Angry thoughts, as other vain thoughts,
may crowd into the heart upon a sudden surprise, but
meekness will not suffer them to lodge there (Jer. 4:14),
nor let the sun go down upon the wrath (Eph. 4:26), for
if it do, there is danger lest it rise bloody the next morning.
Anger concocted, becomes malice; it is the wisdom of meekness, by proper applications, to disperse the humor before

it comes to a head. One would have thought when David so deeply resented Nabal's abuse, that nothing less than the blood of Nabal and all his house could have quenched his heat, but it was done at a cheaper rate; and he showed his meekness by yielding to the diversion that Abigail's present and speech gave him, and that with satisfaction and thankfulness. He was not only soon pacified, but blessed her, and blessed God for her that pacified him. God does not "contend for ever," neither is he "always wroth"; his "anger endures but a moment" (Psalm 30:5). How unlike then are those to him whose sword devours forever, and whose anger burns like the coals of juniper. But the grace of meekness, if it fail of keeping the peace of the soul from being broken, yet fails not to recover it presently, and to make up the breach, and upon the least transport steps in with help in the time of need, restores the soul, and puts it in frame again, and no great harm is done. Such as these are the achievements of meekness as it governs our own anger.

b. *Meekness teaches and enables us patiently to bear the anger of others*, which property of meekness we have special occasion for in reference to our superiors and equals. Commonly, that which provokes anger is anger, as fire kindles fire; now meekness prevents that violent collision which forces out these sparks, and softens at least one side, and so puts a stop to a great deal of mischief; for it is the second blow that makes the quarrel. Our first care should be to prevent the anger of others by giving no offence to any, but becoming all things to all men; everyone studying to "please his neighbor for good to edification" (Rom. 15:2), and endeavoring as much as lies in us to accommodate ourselves to the temper of all with whom we have to do and to make ourselves acceptable and agreeable to them. How easy and comfortable should we make every relation and all our intercourse if we were but better acquainted with this art of obliging. Naphtali's tribe, that was famous for giving *goodly words* (Gen. 49:21), had the happiness of being "satisfied with favor" (Deut. 33:33), for "every man shall kiss his lips that giveth a right answer" (Prov. 24:26). In the conjugal relation it is taken for granted (1 Cor. 7:33, 34) that the care of the husband is to "please his wife" and the care of the wife is to "please her husband"; and where there is that mutual care, comfort cannot be wanting. Some people love to be unkind and take pleasure in displeasing, and especially contrive to provoke those they find passionate and easily provoked that (as he that giveth his "neighbor drink, and putteth his bottle to him," Hab. 2:15, 16) they may look upon his shame to which in his passion he exposes himself, and so they make a mock at sin, and become like the madman that casts firebrands, arrows, and death, and says, "Am not I in sport?" But the law of Christ forbids us to "provoke one another" (Gal. 5:26) unless it be to "love and to good works," and enjoins us to "bear one another's burdens, and so to fulfil the law of Christ."

But because they must rise betimes, who will please everybody, and carry their cup even indeed; who will give no offence; our next care therefore must be so to behave ourselves when others are angry that we may not make bad worse. And this is one principal thing in which the younger must submit themselves to the elder; nay, in which all of us must be subject one to another, as our rule is. And here meekness is of use either to enjoin silence, or to indite a soft answer.

(1) *To enjoin silence.* It is prescribed to servants to "please their masters well in all things," not "answering again," for that must needs be displeasing (Tit. 2:9); better say nothing than say that which is provoking. When our hearts are hot within us it is good for us to keep silence

and hold our peace; so David did (Psalm 39:3) and when he did speak it was in prayer to God and not in reply to the wicked that were before him." If the heart be angry, angry words will but inflame it the more, as wheels are heated by a rapid motion. One reflection and repartee begets another, and the beginning of the debate is like the letting forth of water which is with difficulty stopped when the least breach is made in the dam; therefore meekness says, "By all means keep silence, and leave it off before it be meddled with." When a fire is begun it is good, if possible, to smother it, and so prevent its spreading. Let us deal wisely and stifle it in the birth, lest afterward it prove too strong to be dealt with. Anger in the heart is like those books which were stored in cellars in the conflagration of London, which though they were extremely heated yet never took fire till they took air many days after, where giving vent to the heat put them into a flame. When the spirits are in a ferment, though it may be some present pain to check and suppress them, and the headstrong passions hardly admit the bridle, yet afterward it will be no grief of heart to us.

Those who find themselves wronged and aggrieved think they may have permission to speak, but it is better to be silent than to speak amiss and make work for repentance. At such a time, he that holds his tongue holds his peace; and if we soberly reflect we shall find we have been often the worse for our speaking, but seldom the worse for our silence. This must be especially remembered and observed by as many as are under the yoke, who will certainly have most comfort in meekness and patience and silent submission, not only to the good and gentle, but also to the froward. It is good in such cases to remember our place and ("if the spirit of a ruler rise up against us") not to *leave* it, that is, not to do anything unbecoming, for yielding "pacifieth great offences" (Eccl. 10:4). We have a common proverb that teaches us this, "When thou art the hammer, knock thy fill; but when thou art the anvil, lie thou still;" for it is the posture thou art cut out for, and which best becomes thee.

If others be angry at us without cause, and we have ever so much reason on our side, yet oftentimes it is best to adjourn our own vindication, though we think it necessary, till the passion be over; for there is nothing said or done in passion but it may be better said and better done afterwards. When we are calm, we shall be likely to say it and do it to a better purpose. A needful truth, spoken in a heat, may do more hurt than good, and offend rather than satisfy. The prophet himself forbore even a message from God when he saw Amaziah in a passion (2 Chron. 25:16). Sometimes it may be advisable to get someone else to say that for us, which is to be said, rather than say it ourselves. However, we have a righteous God to whom (if, in a meek silence, we suffer ourselves to be run down unjustly) we may "commit our cause," and having his promise that he will "bring forth our righteousness as the light, and our judgment as the noonday" (Psalm 37:6), we had better leave it in his hands than undertake to manage it ourselves, lest that which we call clearing ourselves, God should call quarrelling with our brethren. David was greatly provoked by those that sought his hurt, and spake mischievous things against him, and yet (says he), "I as a deaf man heard not, I was a dumb man that openeth not his mouth" (Psalm 38:13). And why so? It was not because he wanted something to say, or because he knew not how to say it, but because "in thee, O Lord, do I hope, thou wilt hear, O Lord my God." If God hear, what need have I to hear? *His* concerning himself in the matter supersedes *ours;* and he is not only engaged in justice to own every right-

eous cause that is injured, but he is further engaged in honor
to appear for those who, in obedience to the law of meekness, commit their cause to him, and trust him with it.
If there is any vindication or avenging necessary (which
Infinite Wisdom is the best judge of) he can do it better
than we can; and therefore "give place unto wrath" (Rom.
12:19), that is, to the judgment of God, which is according
to truth and equity; make room for him to take the seat,
and do not you step in before him. It is fit that our wrath
should stand by to give way to his, for the "wrath of man"
engages not the "righteousness of God" for him (James 1:20).
Even just appeals made to him, if they be made in passion,
are not admitted into the court of heaven, being not duly
put in; that one thing, error, is sufficient to overrule them.
Let not therefore those that do well and suffer for it spoil
their own vindication by mistiming and mismanaging it;
but tread in the steps of the Lord Jesus "who, when he
was reviled, reviled not again; when he suffered, he threatened not, but was as a lamb dumb before the shearers";
and so "committed himself to him that judges righteously."
It is indeed a great piece of self-denial to be silent when we
have enough to say, and provocation to say it; but if we do thus
control our tongues, out of a pure regard for peace and love,
it will turn to a good account and will be an evidence for
us that we are Christ's disciples, having learned to deny
ourselves. It is better by silence to yield to our brother,
who is, or has been, or may be, our friend, than by angry
speaking to yield to the devil, who has been, and is, and
ever will be, our sworn enemy.

(2) *To indite a soft answer.* This Solomon commends
as a proper expedient to turn away wrath, while grievous
words do but stir up anger. When any speak angrily to us,
we must pause a while, and study an answer, which, both
for the matter and manner of it, may be mild and gentle.

This brings water, while peevishness and provocation would but bring oil to the flame. Thus is death and life in the power of the tongue; it is either healing or killing, an antidote or a poison, according as it is used. When the waves of the sea beat on a rock, they batter and make a noise; but a soft sand receives them silently, and returns them without damage. A soft tongue is a wonderful medicine, and has a very strange virtue in it; for Solomon says, "It breaks the bone" (Prov. 25:15), that is, it qualifies those that were provoked, and makes them pliable; it heaps "coals of fire" upon the head of an enemy, not to burn him, but to melt him (Prov. 25:21, 22). "Hard words break no bones," we say, but it seems soft ones do (and yet do no harm), as they calm an angry spirit, and prevent its progress, breaking it as we do a flint upon a cushion. A stone that falls on a wool-pack rests there, and rebounds not to do any further mischief, such is a meek answer to an angry question. It is observed in that encounter between the royal tribe and the other ten that the "words of the men of Judah were fiercer than the words of the men of Israel" (2 Sam. 19:43). When passion is up that God whose eyes are upon all the ways of men takes notice who speaks fiercely and sets a mark upon them.

The good effects of a soft answer and the ill consequence of a peevish one are observable in the stories of Gideon and Jephtha. Both of them in the day of their triumphs over the enemies of Israel were causelessly quarrelled with by the Ephraimites (an angry sort of people it seems, who took it very heinously when the danger was past and the victory won that they had not been called upon to engage in the battle). Gideon pacified them with a soft answer, "What have I done now in comparison of you?" (Judges 8:2), magnifying their achievements and lessening his own, speaking honorably of them, and meanly of himself, "Is not the gleaning of the grapes of Ephraim better than the vintage of Abiezar?" In which reply it is hard to say whether there was more of wit or wisdom: and the effect was very good. The Ephraimites were pleased, their anger turned away, a civil war prevented, and nobody could think the worse of Gideon for his mildness and self-denial. On the contrary, he won more true honor by this victory over his own passion than he did by his victory over all the host of Midian; for he that "hath rule over his own spirit, is better than the mighty" (Prov. 16:32). The Angel of the Lord has pronounced him a "mighty man of valor" (Judges 6:12) and his tame submission did not at all derogate from that part of his character. But Jephtha, who by many instances appears to be a man of a rough and hasty spirit, though enrolled among the eminent believers (Heb. 11:32), for all good people are not alike happy in their temper, when the Ephraimites in like manner pick a quarrel with him, rallies them, upbraids them with their cowardice, boasts of his own courage, challenges them to make good their cause (Judges 12:2, 3). They retort a scurrilous reflection upon Jephtha's country (as it is usual with passion to taunt and jeer one another), "Ye Gileadites are fugitives" (Judges 12:4). From words they go to blows, and so great a matter does this little fire kindle that there goes no less to quench the flame than the blood of two and forty thousand Ephraimites. All which had been happily prevented if Jephtha had had but half as much meekness in his heart as he had reason on his side.

A soft answer is the dictate and dialect of that wisdom which is from above, which is "peaceable, gentle, and easy to be entreated." And to recommend it to us we have the pattern of good men as that of Jacob's behavior to Esau; though who is so hard to be won as a brother offended, yet as he had prevailed with God by faith and prayer, so he prevailed with his brother by meekness and humility. We have also the pattern of good angels, who, even when a rebuke was needful, dared not turn it into a railing accusation, dared not give any reviling languague, not to the devil himself, but referred the matter to God, "The Lord rebuke thee," as that passage in Jude 9 is commonly understood. Nay, we have the pattern of a good God who, though he could plead against us with his great power, yet gives soft answers: witness his dealing with Cain when he was wroth and his countenance fallen, reasoning the case with him, "Why art thou wroth. . . . If thou doest well, shalt not thou be accepted?" (Gen. 4:6, 7). With Jonah likewise, when he was so discontented: "Doest thou well to be angry?" (Jonah 4:4, 9). This is represented in the parable of the prodigal son by the action of the father towards the elder brother who was so angry that he would not come in. The father did not say, "Let him stay out then," but he came himself and entreated him (when he might have interposed his authority, and commanded him), and said, "Son, thou art ever with me" (Luke 15:28, 31). When a passionate parley is begun, there is a plague broke out; the meek man, like Aaron, takes his censer with the incense of a soft answer, steps in seasonably, and stays the plague.

This soft answer, in case we have committed a fault (though perhaps not culpable to that degree that we are charged with), must be penitent, humble, and submissive, and we must be ready to acknowledge our error, and not stand in it, or insist upon our own vindication, but rather aggravate than excuse it, rather condemn than justify ourselves. It will be a good evidence of our repentance toward God to humble ourselves to our brethren whom we have offended, as it will be also a good evidence of our being forgiven of God if we be ready to forgive those that have offended us: and such yielding pacifies great offences. Meekness teaches us, as often as we traspass against our brother, to turn again and say, "I repent" (Luke 17:4). An acknowledgement in case of a wilful affront is perhaps as necessary to pardon as, we commonly say, restitution is in case of wrong. And so much for the opening of the nature of meekness, which yet will receive further light from what follows.

II. *We must be of a quiet spirit.*

Quietness is the evenness, the composure, and the rest of the soul, which speaks both the nature and the excellency of the grace of meekness. The greatest comfort and happiness of man is sometimes set forth by quietness. That peace of conscience which Christ has left for a legacy to his disciples, that present sabbatism of the soul, which is an earnest of the rest that remains for the people of God, is called "quietness and assurance forever," and is promised as "the effect of righteousness" (Isa. 32:17), and it follows, "My peace shall dwell in quiet resting-places." So graciously has God been pleased to entwine interests with us, as to enjoin the same thing under the notion of a duty which he proposes and promises under the notion of a privilege. Justly may we say that we serve a good Master, whose "yoke is easy" (Matt. 11:30). It is *Chrestos,* not only easy but *sweet* and *gracious* (so the word signifies), not only tolerable, but amiable: "Wisdom's ways" are not only pleasant, but pleasantness itself, and all her "paths are peace" (Prov. 3:17). It is the character of the Lord's people, both in respect of holiness and happiness that, however they be branded as the troublers of Israel, they are the "quiet in the land" (Psalm 35:20). If every saint be made a spiritual prince (Rev. 1:6), having a dignity above others, and a dominion over himself, surely he is like that Seraiah, a "quiet prince" (Jer. 51:59). It is a reign with Christ, the transcendent Solomon, under the influence of whose golden sceptre there is abundance of peace "as long as the moon endures," yea, and longer, "for, of the increase of his government and peace there shall be no end." Quietness is in the text recommended to us as a grace which we should be endued with, and as a duty which we should practise. In the midst of all the affronts and injuries that are or can be offered us, we must keep our spirits sedate, and undisturbed, and evidence by a calm and even and regular behavior that they are so. This is quietness. Our Savior has pronounced the blessing of adoption upon the peacemakers (Matt. 5:9), as David professes himself to be (Psalm 120:7), in opposition (such an opposition as meekness is capable of) to those that "delight in war" (Psalm 68:30). Now if charity be for peace-making, surely this "charity begins at home," and is for making peace there in the first place. Peace in our own souls is some conformity to the example of the God of peace who, though he does not always give peace on this earth, yet evermore "makes peace in his own high-places" (Job 25:2). This, some think, is the primary intention of that peace-making on which Christ here commands the blessing: it is to have strong and hearty affections to peace, to be peaceably-minded; for *making* in Scripture notes the bent and inclination of the soul: as to make a lie is to be given to lying; so to make peace is to be addicted to peace; to have a disposition in the soul ready to command the peace when there is at any time any kind of disturbance. In a word, quietness of spirit is the soul's stillness and silence from intending provocation *to,* or resenting provocation *from,* any with whom we have to do.

The word has something in it of a metaphor which we would not choose but fairly prosecute, for the illustration of the grace of meekness.

1. *We must be quiet as the air is quiet from winds.* Disorderly passions are like stormy winds in the soul; they toss and hurry it, and often split or strand or overset it; they move it "as the trees of the wood are moved with the wind" (Isa. 7:2); it is the prophet's comparison, and it is an apt emblem of a man in passion. Now meekness restrains these winds, says to them, "Peace, be still," and so preserves a calm in the soul and makes it conformable to him who has the winds in his hands, and is herein to be praised that even the stormy winds fulfil his word. A brisk gale is often useful, especially to the "ships of desire" (Job 9:26); so there should be in the soul such a warmth and vigor as will help to speed us to the desired harbor. It is not well to lie wind-bound in dulness and indifference: but tempests are perilous, yea, though the wind be in the right point; so are strong passions, even in good men, they both hinder the voyage and hazard the ship: such a quickness as consists with quietness is what we should all labor after, and meekness will contribute very much toward it. Meekness will silence the noise, control the force, moderate the impetus, and correct all undue and disorderly transports. What manner of grace is this that even the winds and the sea obey it? If we will but use the authority God has given over our own hearts, we may keep the winds of passion under the command of religion and reason, and then the soul is quiet, the sun shines, all is pleasant, serene, and smiling, and the man sleeps sweetly and safely on the lee-side. We make our voyage among rocks and quicksands, but if the weather be calm we can the better steer so as to avoid them, and by a due care and temper hit the mean between extremes; whereas he that suffers these winds of passion to get head, and spread a large sail before them, while he shuns one rock splits upon another, and is in danger of being drowned in destruction and perdition by many

foolish and hurtful lusts, especially those whence "wars and fightings come."

2. *We must be quiet as the sea is quiet from waves.* The wicked, whose sin and punishment both lie in the unruliness of their own souls, and the violence and disorder of of their own passions, which perhaps will not be the least of their eternal torments, are compared "to the troubled sea, when it cannot rest, whose waters cast forth mire and dirt" (Isa. 57:20); that is, they are uneasy to themselves, and to all about them, "raging waves of the sea" (Jude, v. 13), "foaming out their own shame"; their "hard speeches" (v. 15) which they speak against God, and "dignities" (v. 8), and "things which they know not" (v. 10), their "great swelling words" (v. 16) and "mockings" (v. 18); these are the shame they foam out. Now meekness is the grace of the Spirit that "moves upon the face of the waters," and quiets them, smooths the ruffled sea and stills the noise of it (it is now *mare pacificum* — the pacific ocean); it casts forth none of the mire and dirt of passion. The waves mount not up to the heaven in proud and vain-glorious boastings; go not down to the depths to scrape up vile and scurrilous language; no reeling to and fro, as men overcome with drink, or with their own passion, which is all one (for if "wine be a mocker" and "strong drink raging" as is said in Proverbs 20:1, anger is no less so), none of that transport which brings them to their wits' end. I refer to the Psalmist's description of a storm in Psalm 107:26, 27, and to what follows there in verse 30: "They are glad because they are quiet, so he bringeth them to their desired haven." This calmness and evenness of spirit makes our passage over the sea of this world safe and pleasant, quick and speedy towards the desired harbor, and is amiable and exemplary in the eyes of others. Such a path does the meek and quiet

Christian make to shine after him, that one would think the deep to be hoary.

3. *We must be quiet as the land is quiet from war.* It was the observable felicity of Asa's reign that in his days "the land was quiet" (2 Chron. 14:1, 5). In the preceding reigns there was "no peace to him that went out, or to him that came in," whether outward bound or homeward bound they were exposed to "great vexations," but now the rumors and alarms of war were stilled, and the people "delivered from the noise of archers at the place of drawing waters," as when the land had rest in Deborah's time (Judges 5:11). Such a quietness there should be in the soul, and such a quietness there will be where meekness sways the sceptre. A soul inflamed with wrath and passion upon all occasions is like a kingdom embroiled in war, in a civil war, subject to continual frights, and losses, and perils; deaths and terrors in their most horrid shapes walk triumphantly, sleeps disturbed, families broken, friends suspected, enemies feared, laws silenced, commerce ruined, business neglected, cities wasted; such heaps upon heaps does ungoverned anger lay when it is let loose in the soul. But meekness makes these wars to cease, breaks the bow, cuts the spear, sheaths the sword, and in the midst of a contentious world preserves the soul from being the seat of war and makes peace in those borders. The rest of the soul is not disturbed; its comforts not plundered, its government not disordered; the laws of religion and reason rule, and not the sword; the trading duties are not interrupted, neither its communion with God, nor its communion with the saints intercepted; no breaking in of temptation, no going out of corruption, no complaining in the streets, no occasion given, no occasion taken, to complain. "Happy is the soul that is in such a case" (Psalm 144:14, 15). "The words of such wise men are heard in quiet, more than the cry of him that ruleth

among fools, and this wisdom is better than weapons of war"
(Eccl. 9:17, 18). This is the quietness we should every
one of us labor after, and it is what we might attain to if we
would but more support and exercise the authority of our
graces (which are as the commissioners of the peace), and
guide and control the power of our passion (which are as
the commissioners of array), in our souls.

4. *We must be quiet as the child is quiet after weaning.*
It is the Psalmist's comparison, "I have behaved" (or rather,
I have *composed*, as Ainsworth translates it) "and quieted
myself" (*my soul*, Heb., for our souls are ourselves, and our
principal care must be concerning them), "as a child is
weaned of his mother, my soul is even as a weaned child"
(Psalm 131:2). A child while it is in the weaning perhaps
is a little cross and froward, and troublesome for a time;
but when it is perfectly weaned how quickly does it forget
the breast and accommodate itself to its new way of feeding.
Thus a quiet soul, if provoked by the denial or loss of some
creature-comfort or delight that has been dear, quiets itself
and does not fret at it, nor perplex itself with anxious cares
how to live without it, but composes itself to make the best
of that which is. If wormwood be put upon the breasts,
which we have called the breasts of consolation, it is but to
make us indifferent to them, and we must set ourselves
to answer that intention, and sit loose to them accordingly.
And this holy indifference to the delights of sense is, like
the weaning of a child, a good step taken towards the "perfect man, the measure of the stature of the fulness of
Christ." A child newly weaned is free from all the uneasi-
ness and disquietude of care and fear and envy and anger
and revenge: how undisturbed is its sleep, and even in its
dreams it looks pleasant and smiling. How easy are its days.
How quiet are its nights. If put into a little temper now
and then how soon is it over, the provocation forgiven, the

sense of it forgotten, and both buried in an innocent kiss. Thus, if ever we would enter into the kingdom of heaven, we must be converted from pride, envy, ambition, and strife for precedency, and must "become like little children." So our Savior, who, even after his resurrection, is called "The Holy Child Jesus" (Acts 4:27) has told us (Matt. 18:3). And even when we have put away other childish things, yet still in "malice" we must be children (1 Cor. 14:20). And as for the quarrels of others, in all broils and heats a meek and quiet Christian endeavors to be as disinterested and as little engaged as a weaned child in the mother's arms who is not capable of such angry resentments.

This is that meekness and quietness of spirit which is here recommended to us, such a command and composure of the soul that it be not unhinged by any provocation whatsoever, but all its powers and faculties preserved in due temper for the just discharge of their respective offices (Col 3:8). In a word, "Put off all wrath, and anger and malice" (those corrupted limbs of the old man), pluck up and cast away those roots of bitterness, and stand upon a constant guard against all the exorbitances of your own passion, and then you will soon know, to your comfort, better than I can tell you what it is to be of a meek and quiet spirit.

The Excellency of Meekness
and Quietness of Spirit

2

The Excellency of Meekness and Quietness of Spirit

THE very opening of this cause, one would think, were enough to carry it, and the explaining of the nature of meekness and quietness should suffice to recommend it to us: such an amiable sweetness does there appear in it, upon the very first view, that if we look upon its beauty we cannot but be enamored with it. But because of the opposition that there is in our corrupt hearts to this, as well as to the other graces of the Holy Spirit, I shall endeavor more particularly to show the excellency of it that we may be brought, if possible, to be in love with it and to submit our souls to the charming power of it.

It is said that "A man of understanding is of an excellent spirit" (Prov. 17:27). He is *frigidus spiritu,* according to Tremellius; he is of a *cool spirit.* Put these together and we learn that a cool spirit is an excellent spirit, and that he is "a man of understanding" who is governed by such a spirit. The text tells us (what need we more) that "it is in the sight of God of great price," and we may be sure that is precious indeed which is so in God's sight; that is good, very good, which he pronounces so, for his judgment is according to truth, and sooner or later he will bring all the world to be of his mind: for as he had decided it, so shall our doom be, and he will be justified when he speaketh, and clear when he judgeth."

The excellency of a meek and quiet spirit will appear if we consider the credit of it, and the comfort of it, and the preparedness there is in it for something further.

I. *Consider how creditable a meek and quiet spirit is.*

Credit or reputation is a thing which most people are very sensibly touched with the ambition of, though few consider aright either what it is, or what is the right way of obtaining it, and particularly it is little believed what a great deal of true honor there is in the grace of meekness, and what a sure and ready way mild and quiet souls take to gain the good word of their Master, and of all their fellow-servants, who love our Master, and are like him.

Let us see what credit there is in meekness:

1. *There is in it the credit of a victory.* What a great figure do the names of high and mighty conquerors make in the records of fame! How are their conduct, their valor, and success cried up and celebrated. But if we will believe the word of truth and pass a judgment upon things according to the rules of it, "He that is slow to anger, is better than the mighty; and he that ruleth his spirit, than he that taketh a city" (Prov. 16:32). Behold, a greater than Alexander or Caesar is here; the former of which, some think, lost more true honor by yielding to his own ungoverned anger than he got by all his conquests. No triumphant chariot so easy, so safe, so truly glorious, as that in which the meek and quiet soul rides over all the provocations of an injurious world with a gracious unconcernedness: no train so splendid, so noble, as that train of comforts and graces which attend this chariot. The conquest of an unruly passion is more honorable than that of an unruly people, for it requires more true conduct. It is easier to kill an enemy without, which may be done at a blow, than to chain up and govern an enemy within, which requires a

constant, even, steady hand, and a long and regular management. It was more to the honor of David to yield himself
conquered to Abigail's persuasions than to have made himself a conqueror over Nabal and all his house. A rational
victory must needs be allowed more honorable to a rational
creature than a brutal one. This is a cheap, safe, and
unbloody conquest that does nobody any harm, no lives, no
treasures are sacrificed to it, the glory of these triumphs are
not stained as others generally are with funerals. "Every
battle of the warrior is with confused noise, and garments
rolled in blood; but this shall be with burning and fuel of
fire" (Isa. 9:5), as a "Spirit of judgment" and a "Spirit of
burning." Nay, in meek and quiet suffering we are "more
than conquerors through Christ that loved us" (Rom. 8:37),
conquerors "with little loss"; we lose nothing bu the gratify-
ing of a base lust: conquerors with great gain, the spoils
we divide are very rich, the favor of God, the comforts of the
Spirit, the foretastes of everlasting pleasures: these are more
glorious and excellent than the mountains of prey. We
are more than conquerors; that is "triumphers," we live a
life of victory, every day is a day of triumph to the meek
and quiet soul.

Meekness is a victory over ourselves and the rebellious
lusts in our own bosoms; it is the quieting of intestine
broils, the stilling of an insurrection at home, which is
oftentimes more hard to do than to resist a foreign invasion.
It is an effectual victory over those that injure us, and make
themselves enemies to us, and is often a means of winning
their hearts. The law of meekness is, "If thine enemy
hunger feed him; if he thirst" *propina illi,* not only *give him
drink,* which is an act of charity, but *drink with him* in
token of friendship and true love and reconciliation; and
"in so doing thou shalt heap coals of fire upon his head,"
not to consume him, but to melt and soften him, that he

may be cast into a new mold; and thus while the angry
and revengeful man that will bear down all before him with
a high hand is overcome of evil, the patient and forgiving
"overcome evil with good" (Rom. 12:20, 21), and fore-
asmuch as their "ways please the Lord," he makes even
their enemies to be at peace with them" (Prov. 16:7).
Nay, meekness is a victory over Satan, the greatest enemy of
all. What conquest can sound more great than this? It is
written for caution to us all, and it reflects honor on those
who through grace overcome, that "we wrestle not against
flesh and blood, but against principalities and powers, and
the rulers of the darkness of this world" (Eph. 6:12). The
magnifying of the adversary magnifies the victory over him;
such as these are the meek man's vanquished enemies, the
spoils of these are the trophies of his victory. It is the design of the devil, that great deceiver and destroyer of souls,
that is baffled; it is his attempt that is defeated, his assault
that is repulsed by our meekness and quietness. Our Lord
Jesus was more admired for controlling and commanding
the unclean spirits, legions of which some souls are possessed
with, and desperate outrageous work they make; the soul
becomes like that miserable creature who "cried and cut
himself" (Mark 5:3-5), or that who was so often "cast into
the fire, and into the waters" (Mark 9:22). The meek and
quiet soul is through grace a conqueror over these enemies,
their fiery darts are quenched by the shield of faith, Satan
is in some measure trodden under his feet, and the victory
will be complete shortly, when "he that overcometh shall
sit down with Christ upon his throne, even as he overcame
and is set down with the Father upon his throne" where he
still appears in the emblem of his meekness, "a Lamb as it
had been slain" (Rev. 5:6). And upon mount Zion, at the
head of his heavenly hosts, he appears also as a Lamb (Rev.

14: 1). Such is the honor meekness has in those higher regions.

2. *There is in it the credit of beauty.* The beauty of a thing consists in the symmetry, harmony, and agreeableness of all the parts: now what is meekness but the soul's agreement with itself? It is the joint concurrence of all the affections to the universal peace and quiet of the soul, every one regularly acting in its own place and order, and so contributing to the common good. Next to the beauty of holiness, which is the soul's agreement with God, is the beauty of meekness, which is the soul's agreement with itself. Behold how good and how pleasant a thing it is for the powers of the soul thus to dwell together in unity, the reason knowing how to rule, and the affections at the same time knowing how to obey. Exorbitant passion is a discord in the soul; it is like a tumor in the face which spoils the beauty of it: meekness scatters the tumor, binds down the swelling, and so prevents the deformity, and preserves the beauty. This is one instance of the comeliness of grace, through "my comeliness which I had put upon thee," says God to Israel (Ezek. 16:14). It puts a charming loveliness and ambiableness upon the soul, which renders it acceptable to all who know what true worth and beauty is. "He that in righteousness, and peace, and joy in the Holy Ghost," (that is, in Christian meekness and quietness of spirit), "serveth Christ, is acceptable to God and approved of men" (Rom. 14:17, 18). And to whom else can we wish to recommend ourselves?

Solomon (a very competent judge of beauty) has determined that it is a man's wisdom that makes "his face to shine" (Eccl. 8:1), and doubtless the meekness of wisdom contributes as much as any one branch of it to this lustre. We read in Scripture of three whose faces shone remarkably, and they were all eminent for meekness. The face of Moses shone (Exod. 34:30), and he was the meekest of all men on earth. The face of Stephen shone (Acts 6:15), and he it was who in the midst of a shower of stones so meekly submitted, and prayed for his persecutors. The face of our Lord Jesus shone in his transfiguration, and he was the great pattern of meekness. It is a sweet and pleasing air which this grace puts upon the countenance, while it keeps the soul in tune and frees it from those jarring ill-favored discords which are the certain effect of an ungoverned passion.

3. *There is in it the credit of an ornament.* The text speaks of it as an *adorning* much more excellent and valuable than gold, pearls, or the most costly array; much more recommending than all the bravery of the daughters of Zion. It is an adorning to the soul, the principal, the immortal part of the man. That outward adorning does but deck and beautify the body, which at the best is but a sister to the worms and will ere long be a feast for them; but this is the ornament of the soul, by which we are allied to the invisible world. It is an adorning that recommends us to God, which is in his sight of "great price," as the text says, and in that says enough to its praise. Ornaments go by estimation; now we may be sure the judgment of God is right and unerring. Everything is indeed, as it is with God; those are righteous indeed that are righteous before God (Luke 1:6), and that is an ornament indeed which he calls and counts so. It is an ornament of God's own making. Is the soul thus decked? It is he that has decked. "By his Spirit he hath garnished the heavens" (Job 26:13), and by the same Spirit has he garnished the meek and quiet soul. It is an ornament of his accepting (it must needs be so if it be of his own working), for to him who has this ornament more adorning shall be given. He has promised that he will "beautify the meek with salvation" (Psalm

149:4), and if the garments of salvation will not beautify, what will? The robes of glory will be the everlasting orna- ments of the meek and quiet spirits. Thus meekness is an ornament that, like the Israelites' clothes in the wilderness, never waxes old, nor will ever go out of fashion while right reason and religion have any place in the world: all wise and good people will reckon those best dressed that put on the Lord Jesus Christ, and walk with him in the white of meekness and innocency. Solomon in all his glory was not arrayed like one of these lilies of the valleys, though "lilies among thorns."

The same ornament, which in the text is recommended to wives, is by the same apostle recommended to us all, "Yea, all of you be subject one to another" (1 Pet. 5:5); that explains what meekness is. It is the mutual yielding which we owe one to another for edification and in the "fear of God" (Eph. 5:21). This seems to be a hard saying and an impracticable duty. How shall we do it? Why it follows, "Be clothed with humility." We must remember two things. First, the fixedness of this grace. We must gird it fast to us and not leave it to hang loose so as to be snatched away by every temptation. Carelessness is no commendation of the soul's adorning. Watchfulness and resolution in the strength of Christ must tie the knot upon our graces and make them as the girdle that cleaves to a man's loins. Second, the comeliness and ornament of it. We must put it on as a knot of ribbons, as an ornament to the soul. Such is the meekness of wisdom. It gives to the head an "orna- ment of grace" and, what is more, "a crown of glory" (Prov. 1:9 and 4:9).

4. *There is in it the credit of true courage.* Meekness is commonly despised and run down by the grandess of the age as a piece of cowardice and mean-spiritedness, and the evidence of a little soul, and is posted accordingly, while the

most furious and angry revenges are celebrated and applauded under the pompous names of valor, honor, and
greatness. This error arises from a mistaken notion of
courage; the true nature whereof is thus stated by the
ingenious pen of Norris Miscell: "That it is a resolution
never to decline any evil of pain, when the choosing of it,
and the exposing of ourselves to it, is the only remedy
against a greater evil." And, therefore, he that accepts a
challenge and so runs himself upon the evil of sin, which is
the greater evil, only for fear of shame and reproach, which
is the less evil, he is the coward; while he that refuses the
challenge and so exposes himself to reproach for fear of
sin, he is the valiant man. True courage is such a presence
of mind as enables a man rather to suffer than to sin, to
choose affliction rather than iniquity, to pass by an affront
though he lose by it and be hissed at for a fool and a sneak
rather than engage in a sinful quarrel. He that can deny
the brutal lust of anger and revenge, rather than violate
the royal law of love and charity, however contrary the
sentiments of the world may be, is truly resolute and cour-
ageous; the Lord is with thee, thou mighty man of valor.
Fretting and vexing is the fruit of the weakness of women
and children, but much below the strength of a man, especially of the new man that is born from above. When our
Lord Jesus is described in his majesty, riding prosperously,
the glory he appears in is *truth*, and *meekness*, and *righteousness* (Psalm 45:4). The courage of those who overcome this great red dragon of wrath and revenge by meek
and patient suffering and by "not loving their lives unto
the death" (Rev. 12:11) will turn to the best and most
honorable account on the other side of the grave, and will be
crowned with *glory*, and *honor*, and *immortality*; when those
that "caused their terror in the land of the living" fall in-

gloriously and "bear their shame with them that go down to the pit" (Ezek. 32:24).

5. *The credit of a conformity to the best patterns.* The resemblance of those that are confessedly excellent and glorious has in it an excellence and glory. To be meek is to be like the greatest saints, the elders that obtained a good report and were of renown in their generation. It is to be like the greatest angels, whose meekness in their converse with and ministration to the saints is very observable in the Scriptures. Nay, it is to be like the great God himself whose goodness is his glory (who is *Deus optimus,* "the best God," and therefore *maximus,* "the greatest"), who is slow to anger, and in whom "fury is not" (Isa. 27:4). We are then "followers of God, as dear children," when we "walk in love" and are "kind one to another, tender-hearted, forgiving one another" (Eph. 5:1, 2 and 4:2). The more quiet and sedate we are, the more like we are to that God who, though he be nearly concerned in all the affairs of this lower world, is far from being moved by its most violent convulsions and revolutions; but as he was from eternity so he is and will be to eternity infinitely happy in the enjoyment of himself. It is spoken to his praise and glory, "The Lord sits upon the floods" (Psalm 24:10), even when "the floods have lifted up their voices, have lifted up their waves" (Psalm 93:3). Such is the rest of the Eternal Mind that he sits as firm and undisturbed upon the moveable flood as upon the immoveable rock, the same "yesterday, today, and forever"; and the meek and quiet soul that preserves its peace and evenness against all the ruffling insults of passion and provocation does thereby somewhat participate of a "divine nature" (2 Peter 1:4).

Let the true honor that attends this grace of meekness recommend it to us. It is one of those things that are honest and pure, and lovely, and of good report; a virtue that has

a praise attending it (Phil. 4:8). A praise not, perhaps, of
men, but of God (Rom. 2:29). It is the certain way to
get and keep if not a great name, yet a good name; such as
is "better than precious ointment." Though there be those
that trample upon the meek of the earth, and look upon
them as Michal upon David, despising them in their hearts;
yet "if this is to be vile," let us be "yet more vile," and
"base in our own sight," and we shall find, as David argues
there, that there are those of whom we shall be "had in
honor," sooner or later (2 Sam. 6:22), for the word of
Christ shall not fall to the ground, that those who humble
themselves shall be exalted.

II. Consider how comfortable a meek and quiet spirit is.

Inward comfort is a desirable good which has more in
it of reality, and depends less upon opinion than that of
credit: and this is that which meekness and quietness of
spirit has such a direct tendency to, nay, which it carries
along with it. What is true comfort and pleasure but a
quietness in our own bosom? Those are most easy to themselves who are so to all about them; while they that are a
burden and terror to others will not be much otherwise to
themselves. He that would lead a quiet life must lead
a peaceable life (1 Tim. 2:2). The surest way to find
rest to our souls is to learn of him who is meek and lowly
in heart (Matt. 11:29). Let but our moderation be known
unto all men "and the peace of God which passeth all
understanding will keep our hearts and minds" (Phil. 4:5,
7). Quietness is the thing which even the busy, noisy part
of the world pretend to desire and pursue: they will be
quiet, yea, that they will, or they will not endure the least
disturbance of their quietness. But verily they go a mad
way to work, in pursuit of quietness; greatly to disquiet
themselves inwardly, and put their souls into a continual

hurry, only to prevent or remedy some small outward disquietude from others. But he that is meek finds a sweeter, safer quietness, and much greater comfort than that which they in vain pursue. "Great peace have they that love this law of love, for nothing shall offend them" (Psalm 119:165). Whatever offence is intended, it is not so interpreted, and by that means the peace is preserved. If there be a heaven anywhere upon earth, it is in the meek and quiet soul that acts and breathes above that lower region which is infested with storms and tempests, the harmony of whose faculties is like the music of the spheres they talk of, a perpetual melody. "Mercy and truth are met together, righteousness and peace have kissed each other."

A meek and quiet Christian must needs live very comfortably, for he enjoys himself, he enjoys his friends, he enjoys his God, and he puts it out of the reach of his enemies to disturb him in these enjoyments.

1. *He enjoys himself.* Meekness is very nearly allied to that patience which our Lord Jesus prescribes to us, as necessary to the keeping possession of our own souls (Luke 21:19). How calm are the thoughts, how serene are the affections, how rational the prospects, and how even and composed are all the resolves of the meek and quiet soul. How free from the pains and tortures of an angry man, who is disseized and dispossessed even of himself, and while he toils and vexes to make other things his own, makes his own soul not so: his reason is in a mist, confounded and bewildered, cannot argue, infer, or foresee with any certainty. His affections are on the full speed, hurried on with an impetus which is as uneasy as it is hazardous. Who is that good man who is "satisfied from himself" (Prov. 14:14)? Who but the quiet man that needs not go abroad for satisfaction, but having Christ dwelling in his heart by faith has in him that peace which

the world can neither give nor take away. While those that are fretful and passionate rise up early, and sit up late, and eat the bread of sorrow in pursuit of revengeful projects, the God of peace "gives to his beloved" (Jedidijahs, one of Solomon's names, who was a man of peace) "sleep" (Psalm 127:2). The sleep of the meek is quiet, and sweet, and undisturbed: those that by innocency and mildness make themselves the sheep of Christ shall be made to lie down in the "green pastures." That which would break an angry man's heart will not break a meek man's sleep. It is promised that "the meek shall eat and be satisfied" (Psalm 22:26). He has what sweetness is to be had in his common comforts, while the angry man either cannot eat, his stomach being too full and high, as Ahab (1 Kings 21:4), or he eats and is not satisfied unless he can be revenged, as Haman (Esther 5:12, 13). "All this avails me nothing (though it was a banquet of wine with the king and queen) as long as Mordecai is unhanged."

It is spoken of as the happiness of the meek that they "delight themselves in the abundance of peace" (Psalm 37:11). Others may delight themselves in the abundance of wealth; a poor delight that is interwoven with so much trouble and disquietude; but the meek, though they have but a little wealth, have peace, abundance of peace, peace like a river, and this such as they have a heart to delight themselves in; *sat lucis intus* — light enough within, as Ecolampadius said, their souls are a Goshen in the midst of the Egypt of this world. They have a light in their dwelling, when clouds and darkness are round about them: this is the "joy which a stranger doth not meddle with." We may certainly have, and we would do well to consider it, less inward disturbance, and more true ease and satisfaction in forgiving twenty injuries than in avenging one. No doubt Abigail intended more than she expressed when to qualify David, and to pursuade him to pass by the affront which Nabal had given him, she prudently suggested that "hereafter this shall be no grief unto thee, nor offence of heart" (2 Sam. 25:31). Not only so, but it would be very sweet and easy and comfortable in the reflection. Such a rejoicing is it, especially in a suffering-day, to have the testimony of conscience that in "simplicity and godly sincerity, not with fleshly wisdom, but by the grace of God," particularly the grace of meekness, "we have had our conversation in the world," and so have pleased God and done our duty. He did not speak the sense, no not of the sober heathen, that said, *Est vindicta, bonum, vita jucundius ipsa* — Revenge is sweeter than life — for it often proves more bitter than death.

2. *He enjoys his friends.* And that is a thing in which lies much of the comfort of human life. Man was intended to be a sociable creature, and a Christian much more so. But the angry man is unfit to be so, that takes fire at every provocation; fitter to be abandoned to the lions' dens, and "mountains of the leopards," than to "go forth by the footsteps of the flock." He that has "his hand against every man," cannot but have (with Ishmael's character Ishmael's fate) "every man's hand against him" (Gen. 16:12), and so he lives in a state of war. But meekness is the cement of society, the bond of Christian communion; it planes and polishes the materials— of that beautiful fabric and makes them lie close and tight, and makes the living stones which build up a spiritual house to be like the stones of the temple that Herod built all as one stone, whereas "Hard upon hard will never make a wall," as the Spanish proverb is. Meekness preserves among brethren that unity which is like the ointment upon the holy head, and the dew upon the holy hill (Psalm 133: 1, 2). In our present state of perfection there can be no friendship, correspondence, or conversation maintained without mutual allowances; we do not yet dwell with angels or spirits of just men made perfect, but with men subject to like passions.

Now meekness teaches us to consider this, and to allow accordingly; and so distances and strangeness, feuds and quarrels, are happily prevented, and the beginnings of them
crushed by a timely care. How necessary to true friendship
it is to surrender our passions, and to subject them all to the
laws of it, was intimated, perhaps, by Jonathan's delivering
to David his sword and his bow and his girdle, all his military
habiliments, when he entered into a covenant of friendship
with him (1 Sam. 18:3, 4).

3. *He enjoys his God;* and that is most comfortable of
all. It is the quintessence of all happiness, and that without
which all our other enjoyments are sapless and insipid. For
this enjoyment none are better qualified than those who are
arrayed with the "ornament of a meek and quiet spirit, which
is in the sight of God of great price." It was when the Psalmist had newly conquered an unruly passion, and composed
himself, that he lifted up his soul to God in that pious and
pathetic breathing, "Whom have I in heaven but thee? and
there is none upon earth that I desire in comparison of thee"
(Psalm 73:25). We enjoy God when we have the evidencces
and the assurances of his favor, the tastes and tokens of his
love, when we experience in ourselves the communication
of his grace, and the continued instances of his image
stamped upon us, and those that are most meek and quiet
have usually the greatest degree of this. In our wrath and
passion we give place to the devil and so provoke God to
withdraw from us; nothing grieves the Holy Spirit of God,
by whom we have fellowship with the Father, more than
"bitterness, and wrath, and anger, and clamor, and evil
speaking" (Eph. 4:30, 31). But to this man does the God
of heaven look with a peculiar regard, "even to him that is
poor," poor in spirit (Isa. 66:2): *to him that is quiet,* according to the Syriac, *to him that is meek,* according to the
Chaldee. The great God overlooks heaven and earth to give

a favorable look to the meek and quiet soul. Nay, he not only looks at such, but "he dwells with them" (Isa. 57:15), noting a constant intercourse and communion between God and humble souls. His secret is with them; he gives them more grace, and they that thus dwell in love "dwell in God, and God in them." The waters were dark indeed, but they were quiet, when the Spirit of God moved upon them, and out of them produced a beautiful world.

This calm and sedate frame does very much qualify and dispose us for the reception and entertainment of divine visits, and "sets bounds to the mountains" (Exod. 19:12) on which God is to descend that no interruption may break in, and charges the "daughters of Jerusalem" by "the roes and the hinds of the field" (those sweet and gentle and peaceable creatures), "not to stir up or awake our Love till he please" (Song of Solomon 11:7). Some think it was for the quieting and composing of his spirit (which seems to have been a little ruffled) that Elisha called for the minstrel "and then the hand of the Lord came upon him" (2 Kings 3:15). Never was God more intimate with any mere man than he was with Moses, the meekest of all the men on the earth; and it was required as a needful qualification of the high priest who was to draw near to minister that he should have "compassion on the ignorant and on them that are out of the way" (Heb. 5:1, 2). The meek will he guide in judgment with a still small voice, which cannot be heard when the passions are loud and tumultuous. The angry man, when he awakes, is still with the devil, contriving some malicious project; the meek and quiet man, when he awakes, is still with God, solacing himself in his favor. "Return unto thy rest, O my soul," says David (Psalm 116:7), when he had reckoned himself among the simple, that is, the mild, innocent, and inoffensive people. Return to thy Noah, so the word is (for Noah had his name from Rest), perhaps alluding to the rest which the dove found with Noah in the ark when she could find none anywhere else. Those that are harmless and simple as doves can with comfort return to God as to their rest. It is excellently paraphrased by Mr. Patrick, "God and thyself" (my soul) "enjoy; in quiet rest, freed from thy fears." It is said that the "Lord lifteth up the meek" (Psalm 147:6): as far as their meekness reigns, they are lifted up in a sphere perpetually calm and serene. They are advanced indeed that are at home in God, and live a life of communion with him, not only in solemn ordinances, but even in the common accidents and occurrences of the world. Every day is a sabbath day, a day of "holy rest" with the meek and quiet soul, that is, one of the days of heaven. As this grace gets ground, the comforts of the Holy Ghost grow stronger and stronger according to that precious promise, "The meek also shall increase their joy in the Lord, and the poor among men shall rejoice in the Holy One of Israel" (Isa. 24:19).

4. *It is not in the power of his enemies to disturb* and interrupt him in these enjoyments. His peace is not only sweet, but safe and secure: as far as he acts under the law of meekness it is above the reach of the assaults of those that wish ill to it. He "that abides quietly under the shadow of the Almighty, shall surely be delivered from the snare of the fowler" (Psalm 91: 1, 3). The greatest provocations that men can give would not hurt us if we did not, by our own inordinate and foolish concern, come too near them, and within reach of their cannon; we may therefore thank ourselves if we be damaged. He that has learned, with meekness and quietness, to forgive injuries, and pass them by, has found the best and surest way of baffling and defeating them; nay, it is a kind of innocent revenge. It was an evidence that Saul was actuated by another spirit in that, when the children of Belial despised him and brought him no presents (hoping by that contempt to give a shock to his infant

government) "he held his peace," and so neither his soul
nor crown received any disturbance (1 Sam. 10:27).
Shimei, when he cursed David, intended thereby to pour
vinegar into his wounds, and to add affliction to the afflic-
ted; but David, by his meekness, preserved his peace, and
Shimei's design was frustrated. "So let him curse" (2 Sam.
16:10). Alas, poor creature! He hurts himself more than
David who, while he keeps his heart from being tinder to
those sparks, is no more prejudiced by them than the moon
is by the foolish cur that barks at it. The meek man's
prayer is that of David, "Lead me to the rock that is higher
than I" (Psalm 61:2); and there, as Mr. Norris expresses it,
I can

> *Smile to see*
> *The shafts of fortune all drop short of me.*

The meek man is like a ship that rides at anchor, *movetur,
sed non amovetur* — "is moved, but not removed." The
storm *moves* it (the meek man is not a stock or stone under
provocation), but does not *remove* it from its port. It is a
grace that in reference to the temptations of affront and
injury quenches the fiery darts of the wicked (as faith in
reference to temptation in general). It is armor of proof
against the spiteful and envenomed arrows of provocation,
and is an impregnable wall to secure the peace of the soul
there, where "thief cannot break through and steal," while
the angry man lays all his comforts at the mercy of every
wasp that will strike at him.

So that, upon the whole matter, it appears that the ornament of a meek and quiet spirit is as easy as it is comely.

III. *Consider how profitable a meek and quiet spirit is.*

All people are for what they can get; it is that which the
busy world is set upon, "Every one for his gain from his

quarter" (Isa. 56:11). It is for this that they break their sleep and spend their spirits and raise so great a dust. Now it will be to convince such that there really is more to be gotten by meekness and quietness of spirit than by all this hurry and confusion. They readily believe that "in all labor there is profit," but let God himself tell them, "In returning and rest shall ye be saved, in quietness and in confidence shall be your strength." They will not take his word for it, but they say, as it follows there, "No, for we will flee upon horses, and we will ride upon the swift" (Isa. 30: 15, 16). He that came from heaven to bless us has entailed a special blessing upon the grace of meekness, "Blessed are the meek" (Matt. 5:5); and his saying they are blessed makes them so, for those whom he blesses are blessed indeed: "blessed, and they shall be blessed."

Meekness is gainful and profitable, in the first place, as it is the condition of the promise. The meek are therefore blessed "for they shall inherit the earth." This quotation from Psalm 37:11 is almost the only express promise of temporal good things in all the New Testament. Not that the meek shall be put off with the earth only; then they would not be truly blessed, but they shall have that as an earnest of something more. Some read it, "They shall inherit the land," that is, the land of *Canaan*, which was not only a type and figure, but to them that believed a token and pledge of the heavenly inheritance. So that, as Dr. Hammond observes "a double Canaan is thought little enough for the meek man. The same felicity, in a manner, attending him which we believe of Adam, if he had not fallen, a life in Paradise, and then a transplanation to heaven." But besides this, meekness is a branch of godliness which has more than other branches of it, the "promise of the life that now is" (1 Tim. 14:8). "They shall inherit the earth;" the sweetest and surest tenure is that by inheritance which is founded in sonship, that which comes by descent to the heir, the law attributes to the act of God who has a special hand in providing for the meek. They are his children and "if children then heirs." It is not always the largest proportion of this world's goods that falls to the meek man's share, but whether he has more or less, he has it by the best title; not by a common but by a covenant-right; he holds *in Capite* — *in* (Christ) *our Head* — an honorable tenure.

If he has but a little, he has it from God's love and with his blessing, and behold all things are clean and comfortable to him. The wise man has determined it, "Better is a dry morsel and quietness therewith, than a house full of sacrifices with strife" (Prov. 17:1), and "Better is a dinner of herbs where love is, than a stalled ox and hatred therewith" (Prov. 15:17). Be the fare ever so scanty, he that has rule over his own spirit knows how to make the best of them; how to "suck honey out of the rock, and oil out of the flinty rock" (Deut. 32:13). "Blessed are the meek, for they shall *wield* the earth," as Wycliffe's translation has it (as I remember it is quoted in the Book of Martyrs), and very significantly. Good management contributes more to our comfort than great possessions. Whatever a meek man has of this earth he knows how to wield it, to make a right and good use of it; that is all in all. Quiet souls so far inherit the earth that they are sure to have as much of it as is good for them: as much as will serve to bear their charges through this world to a better; and who would covet more? Enough is as good as a feast. The promise of God without present possession is better than possession of the world without an interest in the promise.

Meekness is gainful and profitable, in the second place, as it has in its own nature a direct tendency to our present benefit and advantage. He that is thus wise, is wise for himself, even in this world, and effectually consults his own interest.

Meekness has a good influence upon our health. If envy be the "rottenness of the bones" (Prov. 14:30), meekness is the preservation of them. As the indulging of inordinate appetites towards those things that are pleasing to the flesh, so the indulging of inordinate passions against those things that are displeasing, do in the effect prejudice and injure the very body which they contend so much for. The excesses and exorbitances of anger stir up those peccant humors in the body which kindle and increase wasting and killing diseases; but meekness governs those humors, and so contributes very much to the good temper and constitution of the body. When Ahab was sick for Naboth's vineyard, meekness would soon have cured him. Moses, the meekest of men, not only lived to be old, but was then free from the infirmities of age: "his eye was not dim, nor his natural force abated" (Deut. 34:7), which may be very much imputed to his meekness as a means. The days of old age would not be such evil days if old people did not by their own forwardness and unquietness make them worse than otherwise they would be. Ungoverned anger inflames the natural heat and so begets acute diseases; it dries up the radical moisture and so hastens chronical decays. The body is called the sheath or scabbard of the soul. How often does an envious fretful soul, like a sharp knife, cut its own sheath, and, as they say of the viper's brood, eat its own way out: all which meekness happily prevents.

The quietness of the spirit will help to cool distempering heats; to suppress melancholy vapors; and this, as other of wisdom's precepts, will be "health to the navel, and marrow to the bones; length of days, and long life, and peace

they shall add unto thee: but wrath kills the foolish man"
(Job 5:2).

Meekness has a good influence upon our wealth, the
preservation and increase of it. As in kingdoms, so in
families and neighborhoods, war begets poverty. Many a
one has brought a fair estate to ruin by giving way to the
efforts of an ungoverned anger, that barbarous idol, to
which even the children's portions and the family's main-
tenance are oftentimes sacrificed. Contention will as soon
cloth a man with rags as slothfulness; that, therefore, which
keeps the peace befriends the plenty. It was Abraham's meek
management of his quarrel with Lot that secured both his
own and his kinsman's possessions, which otherwise would
have been an easy prey to the Canaanite and the Perizzite
that dwelt then in the land (Gen. 13:7, 8). And Isaac,
whom I have sometimes thought to be the most quiet and
calm of all the patriarchs, and who passed the days of his
pilgrimage most silently, raised the greatest estate of any of
them (Gen. 26:13). "He grew till he became very great,"
and his son Jacob lost nothing in the end by his meek and
quiet carriage toward his uncle Laban. Revenge is costly;
Haman bid largely for it, no less than ten thousand talents
of silver (Esth. 3:9): it is better to forgive, and save the
charges. Mr. Dod used to say, "Love is better than law; for
love is cheap, but law is chargeable." Those tradesmen are
commonly observed to thrive most who make the least noise,
who work with quietness and mind their own business (2
Thess. 3:12).

Meekness has a good influence upon our safety. In the
day of the Lord's anger the meek of the earth are most likely to be secured. "It may be you shall be hid" (Zeph. 2:3):
if any be, you shall; you stand fairest for special protections.
Meekness approaches to that innocence which is commonly
an effectual security against wrongs and injuries. However

some base and servile spirits may insult over the tame and
humble; yet with all persons of honor, it is confessedly a
piece of cowardice to set upon an unarmed, unresisting man
who resents not provocation. "Who is he that will harm
you, if you be followers of him that is good?" (1 Pet. 3:13).
Who draws his sword, or cocks his pistol at the harmless
silent lamb? But everyone is ready to do it at the furious
barking dog. Thus does the meek man escape many of those
perplexing troubles, those woes, and sorrows, and wounds
without cause which he that is passionate, provoking, and
revengeful pulls upon his own head. Wise men turn away
wrath, but a fool's lips enter into contention, and his mouth
calls for strokes. It is an honor to a man to cease from
strife, but every fool will be meddling to his own hurt. Mr.
Baxter gives an example of this in his book *Obedient Patience*: "That once, going along London streets, a hectoring
rude fellow justled him: he went on his way, and took no
notice of it; but the same man affronting the next he met in
like manner, he drew his sword and demanded satisfaction,
and mischief was done." He that would sleep both in a
whole skin and in a whole conscience must learn rather to
forgive injuries than to revenge them. The two goats that
met upon the narrow bridge, as in the fable, were both in
danger should they quarrel; but were both preserved by the
condescension of one who lay down and let the other go over
him. It is the evil of passion that it turns our friends into
enemies; but it is the excellency of meekness that it turns
our enemies into friends, which is an effectual way of conquering them. Saul, as inveterate an enemy as could be,
was more than once melted by David's mildness and meekness. "Is this thy voice, my son David?" (1 Sam. 24:16). "I
have sinned, return, my son David" (1 Sam. 26: 21). And
after that, Saul persecuted him no more (1 Sam. 27:4).
The change that Jacob's meekness made in Esau is no less

observable; and, some think, is remarked as very strange and surprising by an unusual pointing in the Hebrew text upon Esau's kissing Jacob (Gen. 30:3). There is a point over every letter, to put the reader in mind to take special notice of it. In the ordinary dispensations of Providence some tell us that they have found it remarkably true that in times of public trouble and calamity it has commonly fared best with the meek and quiet; their lot has been safe and easy, especially if compared with the contrary fate of the turbulent and seditious. Whoso is wise and observes these things will understand the loving kindness of the Lord to the quiet in the land, against whom we read indeed of plots laid, and deceitful matters devised (Psalm 33:20); but those by a kind and overruling providence are ordinarily baffled and made unsuccessful. Thus does this grace of meekness carry its own recompense along with it, and in keeping this commandment, as well as after keeping it, there is a "great reward" (Psalm 19:11).

IV. Consider what a preparative it is for something further.

It is a very desirable thing to "stand complete in all the will of God" (Col. 4:12), to be fitted and furnished for every good work, to be made ready, a people prepared for the Lord: a living principle of grace is the best preparation for the whole will of God. Grace is establishing to the heart; it is the root of the matter, and a good foundation for the time to come. This grace of meekness is particularly a good preparation for what lies before us in this world.

1. *It makes us fit for any duty.* It puts the soul in frame and keeps it so for all religious exercises. There was no noise of axes and hammers in the building of the temple: those are most fit for temple service that are most quiet and composed. The work of God is best done when it is done without noise. Meekness qualifies and disposes us to hear and receive the

word. When malice and envy are laid aside, and we are like
new-born babes for innocence and inoffensiveness, then we are
most fit to "receive the sincere milk of the word," and are most
likely to grow thereby (1 Pet. 2: 1, 2). Meekness prepares
the soil of the heart for the seed of the word, as the husband-
man "opens and breaks the clods of his ground, and makes
plain the face thereof," and then "casts in the principal wheat
and the appointed barley" (Isa. 28: 24, 25). Christ's ministers are fishers of men, but we seldom fish successfully in
these troubled waters. The voice that Eliphaz heard was
ushered in with a profound silence (Job 4:16), and in "slum-
berings upon the bed," a quiet place and posture. "God opens
the ears of men, and sealeth their instructions" (Job 33: 15,
16). Prayer is another duty which meekness disposes us for
the right and acceptable performance of. We do not lift up
pure hands in prayer if they be not without wrath (1 Tim.
2:3). Prayers made in wrath are written in gall, and can
never be pleasing to, or prevailing with, the God of love and
peace. Our rule is, "First go and be reconciled to thy brother, and then come and offer thy gift" (Matt. 5: 23, 24).
And if we do not take this method, though we seek God in
a due ordinance, we do not seek him in the due order.

The Lord's day is a day of rest, and none are fit for it but
those who are in a quiet frame, whose souls are entered
into that present sabbatism which the gospel has provided
for the people of God (Heb. 4:9). The Lord's supper is
the gospel-feast of "unleavened bread" which must be kept,
not with the old leaven of wrath, and malice, and wickedness, but with the unleavened bread of sincerity and truth.

God made a gracious visit to Abraham (Gen. 13:14) after Lot was separated from him, that is, after the strife between him and Lot was over, in which he had discovered so
much mildness and humility. The more carefully we preserve the communion of saints, the fitter we are for com-

munion with God. It is observable that the sacrifices which
God appointed under the law were not ravenous beasts and
birds of prey, but calves, and kids, and lambs, and turtle-
doves, and young pigeons, all of them emblems of meekness
and gentleness and inoffensiveness; for "with such sacrifices
God is well pleased." This quietness of spirit contributes
very much to the constant steadiness and regularity of a religious conversation. Hot and eager spirits, that are ready
to take fire at everything, are usually very inconstant in their
profession, and of great inconsistency with themselves, like
a man in an ague fit, sometimes burning hot, and sometimes
shivering for cold; or like those that gallop in the beginning
of their journey, and tire before the end of it. The meek
and quiet Christian, however, is still the same; and, by keeping to a constant rate, rids ground. If you would have one
foot of the compass go even round the circumference, you
must be sure to keep the other fixed and quiet in the center,
for your strength is to sit still.

2. *It makes us fit for any relation* which God in his providence may call us into. Those who are quiet themselves cannot but be easy to all that are about them; and the nearer
they are to us in relation and converse, the more desirable it
is that we should be easy to them. Relations are various, as
superiors, inferiors, and equals; he that is of a meek and quiet
spirit is cut out for any of them. Moses was forty years a
courtier in Egypt, forty years a servant in Midian, and forty
years a king in Jeshurun; and his meekness qualified him
for each of these posts, and still he held fast his integrity.
There are various duties requisite, according as the relation
is, and various graces to be exercised; but this of meekness is
the golden thread that must run through all. If man be a
sociable creature, the more he has of humility, the more fit
he is for society. Meekness would greatly help to preserve
the wisdom and due authority of superiors, the obedience

and due subjection of inferiors, and the love and mutual
kindness and serviceableness of equals. A calm and quiet
spirit receives the comfort of the relation most thankfully,
studies the duty of the relation most carefully, and bears the
inconvenience° of the relation (for there is no unmixed comfort under the sun) most cheerfully and easily. I have heard
of a married couple, who, though they were both naturally
of a hot and hasty temper, yet lived very comfortably in that
relation by observing an agreement made between themselves, "Never to be both angry together." This is an excellent law of meekness which, if faithfully lived up to, would
prevent many of those breaches among relations which occasion so much guilt and grief and are seldom healed without a scar. It was part of the good advice given by a pious
and ingenious father to his children newly entered into
marriage:

> *Doth one speak fire? t'other with water come;*
> *Is one provoked? be t'other soft or dumb.*

And thus *one wise, both happy.* But where wrath and anger are indulged, all relations are embittered, those that
should be helps become as thorns in our eyes, and goads
in our sides. "Two indeed are better than one," and yet it
is better to dwell alone in the wilderness than with a contentious and angry relation "who is like a continual drop-
ping in a very rainy day" (Prov. 21:19; 27:15). Some of
the Hebrew critics have noted that if you take away "the
fear of the Lord" from "husband and wife," there remains
but "fire" and "fire." It is so in other relations.

3. *It makes us fit for any condition* according as the
wise God shall please to dispose of us. Those that through
grace are enabled to compose and quiet themselves are fit
to live in this world, where we meet with so much every

day to discompose and disquiet us. In general, whether the outward condition be prosperous or adverse, whether the world smile or frown upon us, a meek and quiet spirit is neither lifted up with the one, nor cast down with the other, but still in the same poise; in prosperity humble and condescending, the estate rising, but the mind not rising with it; in adversity encouraged and cheered up, "cast down, but not in despair"; in both "even," like a dye, throw in which way you will, it lights on a square side. St. Paul, who had learned in every state to be content, "satisfied within himself, knew how to be abased, and knew how to abound; every where, and in all things, he was instructed both to be full and to be hungry, both to abound, and to suffer need" (Phil. 4: 11, 12). Changes without made none within. It is a temper which, as far as it has the ascendant in the soul, makes every burden light by bringing the mind to the condition, when the condition is not in everything brought to the mind. Prosperity and adversity have each of them their particular temptation to peevishness and frowardness; the former by making men imperious, the latter by making men impatient. Against the assaults of each of these temptations the grace of meekness will stand on guard. Being to pass through this world "by honor and dishonor, by evil report and good report," that is, through a great variety of conditions and treatments, we have need of that long-suffering and kindness, and love unfeigned, which will be the armor of righteousness on the right hand and on the left (2 Cor. 6:6-8). Meekness and quietness will fortify the soul on each hand, and suit it to the several entertainments which the world gives us; like a skilful pilot who, whatever point of the compass the wind blows from, will shift his sails accordingly, and who knows either how to get forward and weather his point with it, or to lie by without damage. It is the continual happiness of a quiet temper to make the best of that which is.

4. *It makes us fit for a day of persecution.* If tribulation
and affliction arise because of the word (which is no foreign
supposition), the meek and quiet spirit is armed for it, so as
to preserve its peace and purity at such a time so that we
may neither torment ourselves with a base fear, nor pollute
ourselves with a base compliance, and these are our two great
concerns. We are accustomed to say, "We will give anything
for a quiet life." I say, anything for a quiet conscience
which will be best secured under the shield of a meek and
quiet spirit "which doth not render railing for railing" (1
Pet. 3:9), nor aggravate the threatened trouble, or represent
it to itself in its most formidable colors; but has learned
to put a *but* upon the power of the most enraged enemies,
saying they can but kill the body; and to witness the most
righteous testimony with meekness and fear (1 Pet. 3:15)
like our Master who "when he suffered, threatened not, but
committed himself to him that judgeth righteously (1 Pet.
2:23). Suffering saints (as the suffering Jesus) are compared to sheep (Isa. 53:7; Rom. 8:36), as sheep dumb before the shearer, nay, dumb before the butcher. The meek
and quiet Christian, if duly called to it, can tamely part not
only with the wool, but with the blood; not only with the
estate, but with the life, and even then rejoice with joy
unspeakable and full of glory. Angry, froward people, in a
day of rebuke, are apt to pull crosses upon themselves by
needless provocations, or to murmur, and complain, and fly
in the face of instruments, and give unbecoming language,
contrary to the laws of our holy religion and the example
of our Master, and so do more hurt than good by their suffering. Whenever we have the honor to be persecuted for
righteousness-sake, our great care must be to glory God, and
to adorn our profession (which is done most effectually by
meekness and mildness, under the hardest censures and the
most cruel usage): so manifesting that we are indeed under

the power and influence of that holy religion which we think it worth our while to suffer for.

5. *It makes us fit for death and eternity.* The grave is a quiet place; "there the wicked cease from troubling" (Job 3:17). Those that were most troublesome are there bound to the peace; and their "hatred and envy (those great make-bates) are there perished" (Eccl. 9:6). Whether we will or will not, in the grave we shall "lie still and be quiet" (Job 3:13). What a great change then must it needs be to unquiet, angry and litigious people! And what a mighty shock will that sudden forced rest give them after such a violent, rapid motion! It is therefore our wisdom to compose ourselves for the grave, to prepare ourselves for it, by adapting and accommodating ourselves to that which is likely to be our long home: this is dying daily, quieting ourselves, for death will shortly quiet us.

The meek and quiet soul is at death let into that rest which it has been so much laboring after; and how welcome must that needs be! Thoughts of death and the grave are very agreeable to those who love to be quiet; for then and there they shall "enter into peace" and "rest in their beds" (Isa. 57:2).

After death we expect the judgment, than which nothing is more dreadful to them that are contentious (Rom. 2:8). The coming of the master brings new terror along with it to those who smite their fellow-servants (Luke 12:45, 46), but those that are meek and quiet are likely to have their plea ready, their accounts stated, and whenever it comes, it will be no surprise to them. To those whose moderation is known to all men it will be no ungrateful news to hear that "the Lord is at hand" (Phil. 4:5). It is therefore prescribed, as that which ought to be our constant care, whenever our master comes we may be found of him in peace (2 Pet. 3:14), that is, in a peaceable temper. "Blessed is that servant, whom his Lord when he comes shall find" in such a frame. "A good man" (says the late excellent Archbishop Tillotson, in his preface to his book *Family Religion*), "would be loath to be taken out of the world reeking hot from a sharp contention with a perverse adversary; and not a little out of countenance to find himself in this temper translated into the calm and peaceable regions of the blessed, where nothing but perfect charity and good-will reigns for ever." Heaven, for certain, is a quiet place, and none are fit for it but quiet people. The heavenly Canaan, that land of peace, would be no heaven to those that delight in war; turbulent and unquiet people would be out of their element like a fish upon dry ground in those calm regions.

They are the sheep of Christ (such as are patient and inoffensive) that are called to inherit the kingdom; "without are dogs" that bite and devour (Rev. 22:15).

They are the wings of a dove, not those of a hawk or eagle, that David would fly upon to his desired rest (Psalm 55:6).

Now lay all this together, and then consider whether there be not a real excellency in this meekness and quietness of spirit which does highly recommend it to all that love either God or themselves, or have any sensible regard to their own comfort either in this world or in that which is to come.

The Application

3

The Application

A. *Have we not reason to lament* the want of "the ornament of a meek and quiet spirit" among those that profess religion, and especially in our own bosoms? If this be Christianity, the Lord help us! How little is there of the thing even among those that make great pretensions to the name. Surely (as one said in another case), *Aut hoc non Evangelium, aut hi non Evangelici* — "Either this is not Gospel, or these are not Gospel-professors." And oh! how bare and uncomely does profession appear for want of this adorning. When the Israelites had stripped themselves of their ornaments to furnish up a golden calf, it is said that they were "made naked to their shame" (Exod. 32: 25). How naked we are (like Adam when he had sinned) for want of this ornament! It is well if it were to the shame of true repentance; for there is reason enough for it.

I am not teaching you to judge and censure others in this matter. There is too much of that to be found among us; we are quick-sighted enough to spy faults in others, the transports of whose passions we should interpret favorably. But we have all cause, more or less, to condemn ourselves, and confess guilt in this matter. In many things we all offend, and perhaps in this, as much as in any, coming short of the law of meekness and quietness.

We are called Christians, and it is our privilege and honor that we are so: we name the name of the meek and lowly Jesus, but how few are actuated by his Spirit, or conformed

to his example! It is a shame that any occasion should be
given to charge it upon professors, who, in other things, are
most strict and sober, that in this they are most faulty; and
that many who pretend to conscience and devotion should
indulge themselves in a peevish, froward, and morose temper and conversation to the great reproach of that worthy
Name by which we are called. May we not say, as that Mo-
hammedan did when a Christian prince had perfidiously
broken his league with him, "O Jesus! are these thy Christians?"

It is the manifest design of our holy and excellent religion to smooth and soften and sweeten our tempers, and
to work off the ruggedness and unevenness of them. Is it
not a wretched thing, therefore, that any who profess it
should be soured and embittered and less conversable and
fit for human society than other people? He was looked
upon as a very good man in his day (and not without cause),
who yet had such an unhappy temper, and was sometimes
so transported with passion, that his friend would say of
him, "He had grace enough for ten men, and yet not enough
for himself." All the disciples of Jesus Christ, even those
of the first three, do not "know what manner of spirit they
are of" (Luke 9:55). So apt are we to deceive ourselves, especially when these extravagances shroud themselves under
the specious and plausible pretence of zeal for God and religion. But yet the fault is not to be laid upon the profession,
or the strictness and singularity of it in other things which
are praiseworthy; nor may we think the worse of Christianity
for any such blemishes. We know very well that "the wisdom that is from above is peaceable, and gentle, and easy to
be entreated," and all that is sweet, and amiable, and en-
dearing, though she is not herein justified of all who call
themselves her children. But the blame must be laid upon
the corruption and folly of the professors themselves, who

are not so perfectly delivered into the mold of Christianity as they should be; but neglect their ornament and prostitute their honor, and suffer the authority of their graces to be trampled upon. They let fire go out of the rod of their branches which devour their fruit: so that there is no meekness as a strong rod, to be a scepter to rule in the soul, which is a lamentation, and shall be for a lamentation (Ezek. 19:14), something resembling the woeful degeneracy of the angels that sinned, of whom it is said that they kept not *Suum principatum* (Jude 6). So the Vulgate might be read, "The government of themselves." They lost the command they should have had over their inferior faculties, and suffered them to get ahead. And is it not much like this when those pretend to the dignity, who have lost the dominion, of a religious profession, having no rule over their own spirits.

And yet, blessed be God, even in this corrupt and degenerate world, there are many who appear in the excellent ornament of a meek and quiet spirit, and some whose natural temper is hasty and choleric (as it is said Calvin's was), yet have been enabled by the power of divine grace to show in a good conversation their works with meekness and wisdom. It is not so impracticable as some imagine to subdue these passions and to preserve the peace of the soul, even in a stormy day.

But that we may each of us judge ourselves, and find matter for repentance herein, I shall only mention those instances of irregular deportment towards our particular relations which evidence the want of "meekness and quietness of spirit."

1. *Superiors are commonly very apt to chide,* and that is for want of meekness. It is spoken to the praise of him who is the great ruler of this perverse and rebellious world that "he will not always chide" (Psalm 103:9). But how

many little rulers are there of families and petty societies that herein are very unlike him, for they are always chiding. Upon every little default, they are put into a fury and transported beyonds due bounds; they are easily provoked either for no cause at all or for very small cause. They are greatly provoked and very outrageous and unreasonable when they are provoked. Their behavior is fiery and hasty; their language is scurrilous and indecent; they care not what they say, nor what they do, nor whom they insult; they are such sons of Belial that a man cannot speak to them (1 Sam. 25:17). One might as well meet a bear robbed of her cubs as meet them. These require meekness, "Husbands should not be bitter against their wives" (Col. 3:17). "Parents should not provoke their children" (Eph. 6:4). "Masters must forbear threatening" (Eph. 6:9). These are the rules; but how few are ruled by them. The undue and intemperate passion of superiors goes under the umbrage and excuse of necessary strictness, and the maintaining of authority, and the education and control of children and servants. But surely every little failure need not be censured. It should rather be passed by, or if the fault must be reproved and corrected, may it not be done without anger? It does not need noise and clamor. Is this the product of a meek and quiet spirit? Is this the best badge of your authority you have to put on? Are these the ensigns of your honor? Is there no other way of making your inferiors know their place but by putting them among the dogs of your flock and threatening them as such? Not that I am against government and good order in families, and such reproofs as are necessary to the support and preservation of it, and those, so sharpened, as some tempers require and call for. But while you are governing others, learn to govern yourselves, and do not disorder your own souls under the pretence of keeping order in your families. Though you yourself may not be aware of it, yet it is certain that by those indications of your displeasure, which transgress the laws of meekness, you do but render yourselves contemptible and ridiculous, and rather prostitute than preserve your authority. Though your children dare not tell you so, yet perhaps they cannot but think that you are unfit to command yourselves. (No one is fit to rule, except he is willing to be governed, said Seneca.) Time was when you were yourselves children, and scholars, and perhaps servants and apprentices: and so, if you will but allow yourselves the liberty of reflection, you cannot but know the heart of an inferior (Exod. 23:9), and should therefore treat those that are now under you as you yourself then wished to be treated. A due expression of displeasure, so much as is necessary to the amendment of what is amiss, will very well consist with meekness and quietness. And your gravity and awful composedness therein will contribute very much to the preserving of your authority, and will command respect abundantly more than your noise and chiding. Masters of families (and masters of schools too) have need, in this matter, to behave themselves wisely (Psalm 101:2), so as to avoid the two extremes: that of Eli's foolish indulgence on the one hand (1 Sam. 2: 23, 24), and that of Saul's brutish rage on the other hand (1 Sam. 20: 30, 33); and for the hitting of this golden mean wisdom is profitable to direct.

2. *Inferiors are commonly very apt to complain.* If everything be not just to their mind they are fretting and vexing, and their hearts are hot within them; they are uneasy in their place and station, finding fault with everything that is said or done to them. A quiet spirit would reconcile us to the post we are in and to all the difficulties of it, and would make the best of the present state though it is attended with many inconveniences. Those unquiet people whom the apostle Jude in his epistle compares to "raging waves of the sea, and wandering stars" (ver. 13), "were murmurers and

complainers" (ver. 16), *blamers of their lot,* as the word
signifies. It is an instance of unquietness to be ever quarrelling with our allotment. Those wives wanted a meek and
quiet spirit who "covered the altar of the Lord with tears"
(Mal. 2:13). Not tears of repentance for sin, but tears of
vexation at the disappointments they met in their outward
condition. Hannah's meekness and quietness was in some
degree wanting when she fretted and wept and would not
eat (1 Sam. 1:7); but prayer composed her spirit and set
her to rights so that "Her countenance was no more sad"
(1 Sam. 1:18). It was the unquietness of the spirit of the
elder brother in the parable that quarrelled so unreasonably
with the father for receiving and entertaining the penitent
prodigal (Luke 15:29). For those that are given to be uneasy, will never want something or other to complain of. It
is true, though not so readily apprehended, that the sullen-
ness and murmuring and silent frets of children aud servants are as great a transgression of the law of meekness as the
more open, noisy, and avowed passions of their parents and
masters. We find the king's chamberlains "wroth with king"
(Esth. 2:21). And Cain's quarrel with God himself for accepting Abel was interpreted as anger at God: "Why art thou
wroth, and why is thy countenance fallen?" (Gen. 4:6).
The sour looks of inferiors are as certain an indication of
anger resting in the bosom as the disdainful looks of superiors; and how many such instances of discontent there
have been, especially under a continual cross, our own consciences may perhaps tell us. It is the want of meekness only
that makes those whom divine Providence has put under
the yoke, children of Belial, that is, impatient of the yoke.

3. *Equals are commonly very apt to clash and contend.*
It is for want of meekness that there are in the church so
many pulpit and paper-quarrels, such strifes of words, and
perverse disputings: that there are in the state such factions

and parties, and between them such animosities and heart-burnings: that there are in neighborhoods such strifes, and brawls, and vexatious law-suits; or such distances, and estrangements, and shyness one of another: that there are in families envies and quarrels among the children and servants, crossing and thwarting, finding fault one with another; and that brethren that dwell together do not, as they should, "dwell together in unity." It is for want of meekness that we are so impatient of contradiction in our opinions, desires, and designs; that we must have our own saying, right or wrong, and everything our own way; that we are so impatient of competitors, not enduring that any should stand in our light, or share in that work of honor which we would engross to ourselves; that we are so impatient of contempt, so quick in our apprehension and resentment of the least slight or affront; and so quick to imagine injuries where really there are none or none intended. They are not only loud and professed contentions, that evidence a want of meekness, but also those silent alienations in affection and conversation which make a less noise; little piques and prejudices conceived which men are themselves so ashamed of that they will not own them: these show the spirit disturbed, and wanting the ornament of meekness. In a word, the wilful doing of anything to disquiet others, slandering, backbiting, whispering, tale-bearing, or the like, is too plain an evidence that we are not ourselves rightly disposed to be quiet.

And now, may we not all remember our faults this day? Instead of condemning others, though ever so faulty, should we not each of us bewail before the Lord that we have been so little actuated by this excellent spirit, and repent of all that which we have at any time said or done contrary to the law of meekness and from under the direction and influence of it? Instead of going about to extenuate and excuse

our sinful passions, let us rather aggravate them, and lay
a load upon ourselves for them, saying as the Psalmist said
when he was recovering from an intemperate heat: "So
foolish have I been, and ignorant, and so like a beast"
(Psalm 73:22). Think how often we have appeared before God and the world without our ornament, without our
livery, to our shame. God kept account of the particular
instances of the unquietness of Israel; they have tempted
me, he says, now these ten times (Num. 14:22). Conscience is God's register that records all our misconduct;
even what we say and do in our haste will not escape observation: let us, therefore, be often opening the book now,
for our conviction and humiliation, or else it will be opened
shortly to our confusion and condemnation. "But if we would
judge ourselves, we should not be judged of the Lord." May
we not all say, as Joseph's brethren did (and perhaps some
are, as they were, in a special manner called to say it, by
humbling providences), "We are verily guilty concerning our
brother" (Gen. 42:21). "Such a time, in such a company,
upon such an occasion, I wanted meekness and was unquiet;
my spirit was provoked, and I spake unadvisedly with my
lips, and now I remember it against myself. Nay, have not
I lived a life of unquietness in the family, in the neighbor-
hood, always in the fire of contention, as in my element, and
breathing threatenings? And by so doing have not I dishonored my God, discredited my profession, disturbed my
soul, grieved the blessed Spirit, and been to many an occasion of sin? And for all this ought not I to be greatly humbled and ashamed?" Before we can put on the ornament of
a meek and quiet spirit we must first wash in the laver of
true repentance, not only for our gross and open extravagances of passion, but for all our neglects and omissions
of the duties of meekness.

B. *Have we not reason to labor and endeavor,* since there is such a virtue and such a praise, to attain these things? Should we not lay out ourselves to the utmost for this "ornament of a meek and quiet spirit?" For your direction in this endeavor (if you be indeed willing to be directed), I shall briefly lay before you five things:

1. Some Scripture-precepts concerning meekness.
2. Some patterns of it.
3. Some particular instances in which we have special need of it.
4. Some good principles that we should abide by.
5. Some good practices that we should abound in, in order to grow in this grace of meekness.

And in opening these things, we will endeavor to keep close to the law and to the testimony.

I. *Some Scripture-precepts concerning Meekness.*

If we lay the word of God before us for our rule, and are ruled by it, we shall find the command of God making meekness and quietness as much our duty as they are our ornament. We are told several specific things.

a. *We must seek meekness.* This command we have, and it is directed to the meek of the earth: "Seek ye the Lord, all ye meek of the earth; Seek meekness" (Zeph. 2:3). Though they were meek, and were pronounced so by him that searches the heart, yet they must seek meekness. This teaches us that those who have much of this grace have need of more, and must desire and seek after more. *Si dixisti, sufficit, peridisti* — "if you say that you have enough, you must perish." He that sits down content with the grace he has, and is not pressing forward toward perfection, and striving to grow in grace, to get the habits of it more strengthened and confirmed and the operations of it more quickened and invigorated, has no true grace at all, it is to be feared. Though he sit ever so

high and ever so easy in his own opinion, he sits down short
of heaven. Where there is life there will be growth, one way
or the other, till we come to the perfect man. "He that hath
clean hands will be stronger and stronger." Paul was a man of
great attainments in grace, and yet we find him forgetting the
things that are behind, and reaching forth to those that are before (Phil. 3:13, 14). Those who took joyfully the spoiling of
their goods are yet told that they have "need of patience" (Heb.
10:34, 36). Thus the meek of the earth (who being on the
earth are in a state of infirmity and imperfection, of trial and
temptation) have still need of meekness; that is, they must
learn to be yet more calm and composed, more steady, and
even, and regular in the government of their passions, and in
the management of their whole conversation. They who have
silenced all angry words must learn to suppress the first risings and motions of angry thoughts.

It is observable that when the meek of the earth are especially concerned to seek meekness, even when the decree
is ready to bring forth, when the day of the Lord's anger
hastens on, when the times are bad, and desolating judgments
are breaking in, then we have occasion for all the meekness
we have, and all we can get, and all is little enough. Meekness toward God the author, and toward men the instruments
of our trouble, meekness to bear the trial, and to bear our
testimony in the trial. There is sometimes an "hour of temptation" (Rev. 3:10), a critical day when the exercise of
meekness is the work of the day. Sometimes the children of
men are more than ordinarily provoking, and then the children of God have more than commonly need of meekness.
When God is justly angry, and men are unjustly angry, when
our mother's children are angry with us, and our Father is
angry too, there is anger enough stirring, and then "Blessed
are the meek" that are careful to keep possession of their souls

when they can keep possession of nothing else, whose hearts
are fixed and quiet in shaking and unquiet times.

Now the way prescribed for the attainment of meekness
is to seek it. Ask it of God, pray for it. It is a fruit of the
Spirit; it is given by the God of all grace, and to him we must
go for it. It is a branch of that wisdom which he that "lacketh
must ask of God," and "it shall be given him" (James 1:5).
The God we address is called "The God of patience and consolation" (Rom. 15:5), and he is therefore the "God of
patience" (for the more patient we are, the more we are com-
forted under our afflictions), and as such we must look to him
when we come to him for grace to make us like-minded, that
is, meek and loving one toward another, which is the errand
the apostle there comes upon to the throne of grace. God's
people are, and should be, a generation of seekers, who covet
the best gifts and make their court to the best giver who never
said to the wrestling seed of Jacob "Seek in vain." Rather he
has given us an assurance firm enough for us to build upon,
and rich enough for us to encourage ourselves with: "Seek
and ye shall find." What would we more? Seek meekness,
and ye shall find it.

The promise annexed is very encouraging to the meek of
the earth that seek meekness: "It may be you shall be hid in
the day of the Lord's anger." Though it be but a promise
with an "it may be," yet it ministers abundance of comfort.
God's probabilities are better than the world's certainties; and
the meek ones of the earth who hope in his mercy and ven-
ture their all upon an intimation of his good-will shall find
to their comfort that when God brings a flood upon the world
of the ungodly he has an ark for his Noahs, his resting, quiet
people, in which they shall be hid, it may be, from the calamity itself. At least they shall be hid from the sting and
malignity of it; "hid" (as Luther said) "either in heaven, or

under heaven, either in the possession, or under the protection, of heaven" (see Psalm 91: 1, 2).

b. *We must put on meekness.* This precept we have: "Put on therefore (as the elect of God, holy and beloved) meekness" (Col. 3: 12) It is one of the members of the new man, which, according to the obligations we lie under from our baptism, we must put on. Put it on as armor, to keep provocations from the heart, and so to defend the vitals. They that have tried it will say it is "armor of proof." When you are putting on the whole armor of God do not forget this. Put it on as attire, as your necessary clothing, which you cannot go without; look upon yourselves as ungirt, undressed, unblest without it. Put it on as a livery-garment, by which you may be known to be the disciples of the meek, and humble, and patient Jesus, and to belong to that peaceable family. Put it on as an ornament, as a robe and a diadem, by which you may be both beautified and dignified in the eyes of others. Put it on as the "elect of God, holy and beloved," because you are so in profession; and that you may approve yourselves so in truth and reality, be clothed with meekness as the "elect of God," a choice people, a chosen people, whom God has set apart for himself from the rest of the world as holy, sanctified to God, sanctified by him. Study these graces which put such a luster upon holiness, and recommend it to those that are without: as beloved, beloved of God, beloved of man, beloved of your ministers; for love's sake put on meekness. What winning persuasive rhetoric is here! Enough, one would think, to smooth the roughest soul and to soften and sweeten the most obstinate heart. Meekness is a grace of the Spirit's working, a garment of his preparing; but we must put it on, that is, we must lay our souls under the commanding power and influence of it. Put it on, not as a loose outer garment, to be put off in hot weather, but let it cleave to us as the girdle cleaves to a man's loins; so put it on as to reckon ourselves naked, to our shame, without it.

c. *We must follow after meekness.* This precept we have: "Thou, O man of God, flee these things, and follow after righteousness, godliness, faith, love patience, meekness" (1 Tim. 6:11). Meekness is here put in opposition to those foolish and hurtful lusts that Timothy must flee from. See what good company it is ranked with. Every Christian is in a sense a man of God (though Timothy is called so as a minister), and those that belong to God are concerned to be and do so, as to recommend themselves to him, and his religion to the world; therefore, let the men of God follow after meekness. The occasions and provocations of anger often set our meekness at a distance from us, and we have it to seek when we have most need of it; but we must follow after it, and not be taken off from the pursuit by any diversion whatsoever. While others are ingenious and industrious enough in following after malice and revenge, projecting and prosecuting angry designs, be you wise and diligent to preserve the peace, both within doors and without. Following meekness bespeaks a sincere desire, and a serious endeavor, to get the mastery of our passion, and to check, govern, and moderate all the motions of it. Though we cannot fully attain this mastery, yet we must follow after it, and aim at it. Follow meekness, that is, "as much as in you lies live peaceably with all men," endeavoring to "keep the unity of the Spirit." We can but make one side of the bargain; if others will quarrel, yet let us be peaceable. If others will strike the fire, that is their fault; let not us be as tinder to it.

d. *We must show all meekness unto all men.* This is one of the subjects which Paul directs a young minister to preach upon: "Put them in mind to show all meekness" (Tit. 3:2). It is that which we have need to be often reminded of. Meekness is here opposed to brawling and clamor, which is the fruit and product of our own anger, and the cause and provocation of the anger of others. Observe, it is *all meekness* that is here recommended to us, *all kinds of meekness;* bearing meekness, and forbearing meekness; qualifying meekness, and condescending meekness; forgiving meekness; the meekness that endears our friends, and that which reconciles our enemies; the meekness of authority over inferiors, the meekness of obedience to superiors, and the meekness of wisdom towards all. *All meekness* is meekness in *all* relations, in reference to all injuries, all sorts of provocation, meekness in all the branches and instances of it; in this piece of our obedience we must be universal. Observe further, we must not only have meekness, all meekness, but we must show it, by drawing out this grace into exercise, as there is occasion: in our words, in our looks, in our actions, in everything that falls under the observation of men, we must manifest that we have indeed a regard to the law of meekness, and that we make conscience of what we say and do when we are provoked. We must not only have the law of love written in our hearts, but in our tongues, too, we must have the law of kindness (Prov. 31:26). And thus the tree is known by its fruit. This light must shine that others may see the good works of it, and hear the good words of it too, not to glorify us, but to glorify our Father. We should study to appear in all our converse so mild, and gentle, and peaceable that all who see us may witness for us that we are of the meek of the earth. We must not only be moderate, but let our "moderation be known" (Phil. 4:5).

He that is in this respect a wise man, let him show it in the meekness of wisdom (James 3:13). What are good clothes worth if they be not worn? Why has the servant a fine livery given him but to show it for the honor of his master and of the family to whom he belongs? How can we say we are meek if we do not show it? The showing of our meekness will beautify our profession, and will adorn the doctrine of God our Savior, and may have a very good influence upon others who cannot but be in love with such an excellent grace, when thus, like the "ointment of the right hand, it betrayeth itself," and the house is filled with the odor of it. Again, this meekness must be thus showed unto all men, foes as well as friends, those without, as well as those within, all that we have anything to do with. We must show our meekness not only to those above us, that we stand in awe of, but to those below us, that we have an authority over. The poor indeed use entreaties, but, whatever is the practice, it is not the privilege of the rich to answer roughly. We must "show our meekness not only to the good and gentle, but also to the froward, for this is thankworthy" (1 Pet. 2:18, 19). Our meekness must be as extensive as our love, so exceeding broad in this commandment, "All meekness to all men." We must show this meekness most to those with whom we most converse. There are some that, when they are in company with strangers, appear very mild and good-humored, their behavior is plausible enough, and complaisant;-but-in-their families they are peevish, and froward, and ill-natured, and those about them scarce know how to speak to them. This shows that the fear of man gives greater check to their passions than the fear of God. Our rule is to be meek toward all, even to the brute creatures over whom we are lords, but must not be tyrants: "a good man is merciful to his beast."

Observe the reason which the apostle there gives why we should "show all meekness toward all men, for we ourselves also were sometimes foolish." Time was, when perhaps we were as bad as the worst of them we are now angry at: and if now it be better with us, we are purely beholden to the free grace of God in Christ that made the difference: and shall we be harsh to our brethren, who have found God so kind to us? Has God forgiven us that great debt, and passed by so many willful provocations, and shall we be extreme to mark what is done amiss against us and make the worst of every slip and oversight? The great gospel argument for mutual forbearance and forgiveness is that God for Christ's sake has forgiven us (Col. 3:13).

It may be of use also for the qualifying of our anger at our inferiors to remember not only our former sinfulness against God in our unconverted state, but our former infirmities in the age and state of inferiors; were not we ourselves sometimes foolish? Our children are careless, and playful, and froward, and scarcely governable, and were not we ourselves so when we were of their age? And if we have now "put away childish things," yet they have not. "Children may be brought up in the nurture and admonition of the Lord without being provoked to wrath."

e. *We must study to be quiet* (1 Thess. 4:11), that is, study not to disturb others, nor to be ourselves disturbed by others; those are quiet that are apt not either to give or take offence. "Be ambitious of this, as the greatest honor, to be quiet," as the word signifies. The most of men are ambitious of the honor of great business, and power, and preferment; they covet it, they court it, they compass sea and land to obtain it: but the ambition of a Christian should be carried out towards quietness. We should reckon that the happiest post, and desire it accordingly, which lies most out of the road of provocation. I cannot avoid mentioning, for the illustration of this, that excellent poem of Lord Hale (the sense of which is borrowed from a heathen).

> *Let him that will ascend the tottering seat*
> *Or courtly grandeur, and become as great*
> *As are his mountain wishes: as for me*
> *Let sweet repose and rest my portion be.*

Let my age
Slide gently by, not overthwart the stage
Of public action, unheard, unseen,
And unconcern'd as if I ne'er had been.

This is studying to be quiet. Subdue and keep under all those disorderly passions which tend to the disturbing and clouding of the soul. Compose yourselves to this holy rest; put yourselves in a posture to invite this blessed sleep which God gives to his beloved. Take pains, as students in arts and sciences do, to understand the mystery of this grace. I call it a mystery because St. Paul, who was so well versed in the deep things of God, speaks of this as a mystery: "I am instructed, as in a mystery, both to be full and to be hungry, both to abound and to suffer need" (Phil. 4:12); that is, in one word, "to be quiet." To study the art of quietness is to take pains with ourselves, to work upon our own hearts the principles, rules, and laws of meekness; and to furnish ourselves with such considerations as tend to the quieting of the spirit in the midst of the greatest provocations. Others are studying to disquiet us; the more need we have to study how to quiet ourselves by a careful watching against all that which is ruffling and discomposing. Christians should, above all studies, study to be quiet, and labor to be actuated by an even spirit under all the unevennesses of Providence; and remember that one good word which Sir William Temple tells us the then Prince of Orange (later King William) said he learned from the master of his ship, who in a storm, was calling to the steersman with this word, "Steady, steady." Let but the hand be steady, and the heart quiet, and then, though our passage be rough, we may make a shift to weather the point, and get safe to the harbor.

II. *Some Scripture-patterns of Meekness and Quietness of Spirit*

Good examples help very much to illustrate and enforce good rules, bringing them closer to particular cases and showing them to be practicable. Precedents are of great use in the law. If we would be found walking in the same spirit, and walking in the same steps with those that are gone before us to glory, this is the spirit we must be actuated by, and these are the steps we must walk in: this is the way of good men, for wise men, to walk in. Let us go forth then by the footsteps of the flock, and set ourselves to follow them who through faith and patience inherit the promises. We are compassed about with a great cloud of witnesses, who will bear their testimony to the comfort of meekness, and upon trial recommend it to us; but we shall single out only some few from Scripture.

a. *Abraham was a pattern of meekness,* and he was "the father of the faithful." The apostle here, in the preceding text, proposes Sarah for an example to women, particularly an example of meekness in an inferior relation. She obeyed Abraham, and, in token of the respect due to a husband, she called him lord. Now Abraham is a pattern of the same grace in a superior. He that was famous for faith, was famous for meekness; for the more we have of faith toward God, the more we shall have of meekness toward all men.

How meek was Abraham when there happened a strife between his herdsmen and Lot's, which, had it proceeded, might have been of ill consequence, for the Canaanite and the Perizzite dwelled then in the land. But it was seasonably taken up by the prudence of Abraham: "Let there be no strife, I pray thee" (Gen. 13:8). Though he might command the peace, yet for love's sake he rather beseeches. Every word has an air of meekness, and a tendency to keep the peace. And when the expedient decided upon for the prevention of strife was their parting from each other, Abraham, though he was the older, quitted his right for the sake of peace and gave Lot the choice, and the gracious visit which God gave him thereupon was abundant recompense for his mildness and condescension. Another instance of Abraham's meekness is in his behavior towards Sarah when she quarreled with him so unreasonably about her maid, angry at that which she herself had the doing of: "My wrong be upon thee . . . . the Lord judge between thee and me" (Gen. 16: 5, 6). Abraham might soon have replied, "You may thank yourself; it was your own doing." But laying aside the present provocation, he abides by one of the original rules of the relation: "Behold, thy maid is in thy hand." He did not answer passion with passion. That would have put all into a flame presently; but he answered passion with meekness, and so all was quiet. Another instance of Abraham's meekness is seen in the transactions between him and Abimelech his neighbor (Gen. 21: 24, 25). He first enters into a covenant of friendship with him, which was confirmed by an oath, and then, though he does not reproach him, reproves him for a wrong that his servants had done him about a well of water. From this incident we learn this rule of meekness: not to break friendship for a small matter of difference. Such and such occasions there are, which they that are disposed to it might quarrel about, but "what is that between thee and me?" If meekness rule, matters in variance may be fairly reasoned and adjusted without violation or infringement of friendship. This is the example of that great patriarch. The future happiness of the saints is represented as the bosom of Abraham (Luke 16:23), a quiet state. Those who hope to lie in the bosom of Abraham shortly, must tread in the steps of Abraham now, whose children we are as long as we thus do well, "and who" (as Maimonides expresses it) "is the father of all who are gathered under the wings of the divine Majesty."

b. *Moses was a pattern of meekness.* It was his master-grace, that in which, more than in any other, he excelled. This testimony the Holy Ghost gives of him: "That the man (Moses) was very meek, above all the men which were upon the face of the earth" (Num. 12:3).

This character of him comes in there in a parenthesis (probably inserted by the same inspired pen that wrote the last chapter of Deuteronomy) upon occasion of an affront he received from those of his own house; which intimates that his quiet and patient bearing of it was, of all others, the greatest proof and instance of his meekness. Those can bear any provocation that can bear it from their near relations. The meekness of Moses, as the patience of Job, was tried on all hands. Armor of proof shall be sure to be shot at. It should seem that his wife was not one of the best-humored women, for what a passion she was in about the circumcising of her son, when she reproached him as a "bloody husband"; and we do not read of one word that he replied, but let her have her saying (Exod. 4: 25, 26). When God was angry, and Zipporah angry, it was best for him to be quiet. The lot of his public work was cast "in the provocation, in the day of temptation in the wilderness" (Psalm 95: 8). But, as if all the mutinies of murmuring Israel were too little to try the meekness of Moses, his own brother and sister (and those of no less a figure than Miriam the prophetess, and Aaron the saint of the Lord), quarrel with him, speak against him, envy his honor, reproach his marriage, and are ready to head a rebellion against him (Num. 12:1, 2). God heard this (ver. 2) and was angry (ver. 9), but Moses, though he had reason enough to resent it wrathfully, was not at all moved by it, took no notice of it, made no complaint to God, no answer to them, and was so little interested in the matter that we do not find one word that he said till we find him praying so heartily for his provoking sister (ver. 13), who was then under the tokens of God's displeasure for the affront she gave him. The less a man strives for himself, the more is God engaged in honor and faithfulness to appear for him. When Christ said "I seek not mine own glory," he presently added "but there is one that seeketh and judgeth." And it was upon this occasion that Moses obtained this good report, "He was the meekest of all the men on the earth." Bishop Hall has said, "No man could have given greater proofs of courage than Moses. He slew the Egyptian, beat the Midianite shepherds, confronted Pharoah in his own court, not fearing the wrath of the king; he durst look God in the face amidst all the terrors of Mount Sinai, and draw near to the thick darkness where God was; and yet that Spirit which made and knew his heart, saith, he was the meekest, mildest man upon the earth. Mildness and fortitude may well lodge together in the same breast, which corrects the mistake of those that will allow none valiant but the fierce."

The meekness of Moses qualified him to be a magistrate, especially to be a king in Jeshurun, among a people so very provoking that they give him occasion to use all the meekness he had, and all little enough, to bear their manners in the wilderness. When they murmured against him, quarrelled with him, arraigned his authority, and were sometimes ready to stone, he resented these provocations with very little of personal application or concern; but instead of using his interest in heaven to summon plagues upon them, he made it his business to stand in the gap, and by his intercession for them to turn away the wrath of God from them; and this not once or twice, but many times.

And yet we must observe that, though Moses was the meekest man in the world, yet when God's honor and glory were concerned, no one was more warm and zealous. Witness his resentment of the golden calf, when in a holy in-

dignation at that abominable iniquity, he deliberately broke
the tables. And when Korah and his crew invaded the
priest's office Moses, in a pious wrath, said unto the Lord,
"respect not thou their offering" (Num. 16: 15). He that
was a lamb in his own cause, was a lion in the cause of
God; anger at sin, as sin, is very well consistent with
reigning meekness. Nor can it be forgotten that though
Moses was eminent for meekness, yet he once transgressed
the laws of it: when he was old, and his spirit was provoked,
he "spake unadvisedly with his lips, and it went ill with
him for it" (Psalm 106: 32, 33). This is written not for
imitation, but for admonition; not to justify our rash anger,
but to engage us to stand upon our guard at all times against
it, in order that he who "thinks he stands, may take heed
lest he fall"; and that he who has thus fallen may not wonder if he come under the rebukes of divine Providence for it
in this world as Moses did, and yet may not despair of being
pardoned upon repentance.

    c. *David was a pattern of meekness,* and it is promised
"That the feeble shall be as" David (Zech. 12: 8). In this,
as in other instances, he was a man after God's own heart.
When his own brother was so rough upon him without
reasons: "Why camest thou down hither?" (1 Sam. 17:28);
how mild was his answer: "What have I now done? Is there
not a cause?" (1 Sam. 17: 29). When his enemies reproached him, he was not at all disturbed at it, "I, as a deaf
man, heard not" (Psalm 38: 13). When Saul persecuted
him with such an unwearied malice, he did not take the
advantage which providence seemed to offer him more than
once to revenge and right himself, but let it to God to do
it for him. David's meek spirit concurred with the proverb
of the ancients, "Wickedness proceedeth from the wicked,
but my hand shall not be upon him" (1 Sam. 24: 13).
When Nabal's churlishness provoked him, yet Abigail's

prudence soon pacified him, and it pleased him to be pacified. When Shimei cursed him with a bitter curse, in the day of his calamity, he resented not the offence, nor would hear any talk of punishing the offender: "So let him curse; let him alone, for the Lord hath bidden him" (2 Sam. 16: 10, 12), quietly committing his cause to God who judges righteously. And other instances there are in his story which evidence the truth of what he said, "My soul is even like a weaned child" (Psalm 131:2). And yet David was a great soldier, a man of celebrated courage, who slew a lion, and a bear, and a Philistine (as much a ravenous beast as either of them); which shows that it was his wisdom and grace, and not his cowardice, that at other times made him so quiet. David was a man that met with very many disquieting and disturbing events in the several scenes of his life, through which, though sometimes they ruffled him a little, yet for the main he preserved an admirable temper, and an evenness and composedness of mind which was very exemplary. When, upon the surprise of a fright, "he changed his behavior before Abimelech, and counterfeited that madness," which angry people realize, yet his mind was so very quiet and undisturbed that at that time he penned the 34th Psalm in which not only the excellency of the matter, and the calmness of the expression, but the composing of it alphabetically (in the Hebrew), speaks him to be even then in a sedate frame, and to have very much the command of his own thoughts. As, at another time, when his own followers spake of stoning him, though he could not still the tumult of his troops, he could those of his spirits, for then he "encouraged himself in the Lord his God" (1 Sam. 30: 6). As to those prayers against his enemies which we find in some of his Psalms, and which, sometimes, sound a little harsh, surely they did not proceed from any such irregular passions as would clash with even

the evangelical laws of meekness. We cannot imagine that
one who was so piously calm in his common conversation
should be sinfully hot in his devotion; nor are these prayers
to be looked upon as the private expressions of David's own
angry resentments; they are to be looked upon as inspired
predictions of God's judgments on the public and obstinate
enemies of Christ and his kingdom. This is made clear by
comparing Psalm 69: 22, 23 with Romans 11: 9, 10, and
Psalm 109:8 with Acts 1:20. Nor are they any more op-
posite to the spirit of the gospel than the cries of the souls
under the altar (Rev. 6: 10), or the triumphs of heaven
and earth in the destruction of Babylon (Rev. 19: 1, 2).

d. *St. Paul was a pattern of meekness.* Though his
natural temper seems to have been warm and eager, which
made him eminently active and zealous, yet that temper was
so rectified and sanctified that he was no less eminently
meek. "He became all things to all men." He studied to
please all with whom he had to deal, and to render himself
engaging to them "for their good to edification." How patiently did he bear the greatest injuries and indignities, not
only from Jews and heathens, but from false brethren that
were so very industrious to abuse and undermine him! How
glad he was that Christ was preached, though out of envy
and ill-will, by those that studied to "add affliction to his
bonds!" In governing the church, he was not led by the
sudden resolves of passion, but always deliberated calmly
concerning the use of the rod of discipline when there was
occasion for it: "Shall I come to you with a rod, or in the
spirit of meekness?" (1 Cor. 4: 21). That is, shall I proceed immediately to censures, or shall I not rather continue
the same gentle usage I have hitherto treated you with, waiting still for your reformation? Herein the spirit of meekness appears more open and legible than in the use of the
rod, though that also is very well consistent with it.

Many other patterns of meekness might be adduced, but the time will fail me to tell of Isaac, and Jacob, and Joseph, and Joshua; of Samuel also, and Job, and Jeremiah, and all the prophets and apostles, martyrs and confessors, and eminent saints, who by meekness subdued, not kingdoms, but their own spirits; stopped the mouths, not of lions, but of more fierce and formidable enemies; quenched the violence, not of fire, but of intemperate and more ungovernable passions; and so wrought righteousness, obtained promises, escaped the edge of the sword, and out of weakness were made strong: and by all this "obtained a good report" (Heb. 11:32-34).

e. *Above all, our Lord Jesus was the great pattern of meekness and quietness of spirit.* All the rest had their spots; the fairest marble had its flaws, but here is a copy without a blot. We must follow the rest no further than they were conformable to this great original: "Be ye followers of me," says Paul, "as I am of Christ" (1 Cor. 11: 1). He fulfilled all righteousness, and was a complete exemplar of all that is holy, just, and good; but I think in most if not all those places of Scripture where he is particularly and expressly propounded to us for an example, it is to recommend to us one or another of the duties of Christianity. Those duties, I mean, which tend to the sweetening of our converse with one another. Therefore was the Word made flesh, and dwelt among us, that he might teach us how to dwell together in unity. We must "walk in love, as Christ loved us" (Eph. 5: 2). "Forgive, as Christ forgave us" (Col. 3: 13). "Please one another, for Christ pleased not himself" (Rom. 15: 2, 3). "Be charitable to the poor, for we know the grace of our Lord Jesus" (2 Cor. 8:9). "Wash one another's feet," that is, stoop to the meanest offices of love, for Christ did so (John 13: 14, Matt. 20: 27, 28). "Doing all with lowliness of mind, for it is the same mind that was in Christ

Jesus" (Phil. 2: 3, 5); and many other the like. But above
all, our Lord Jesus was an example of meekness. Moses had
this grace as a servant, but Christ as a son; he was anointed
with it above measure. He is therefore called "The Lamb
of God," for his meekness, and patience, and inoffensiveness; and even in his exaltation he retains the same character. One of the elders told John "That the lion of the
tribe of Judah would open the sealed book" (Rev. 5: 5);
and, John says, "I beheld, and lo! a Lamb" (Rev. 5:6).
He that was a lion for strength and courage, was a lamb for
mildness and gentleness; and if a lion, yet the lion of the
tribe of Judah which the dying patriarch describes as a lion
"gone up from the prey," and that is "stooped down and
couched, and not to be roused up" (Gen. 49:9); which
speaks the quietness and repose even of this lion. If Christ
be a lion, he is a lion resting. The devil is a lion "roaring"
(1 Pet. 5: 8). But the adorations given to Christ by the
heavenly hosts speak of him as "the Lamb" (Rev. 5: 8, 12,
13). "Blessing and glory — to him that sits upon the
throne.", They do not say, and to the lion of the tribe of
Judah, but "to the Lamb," though he has a name given him
above every name, yet he will be known by that name which
denotes his meekness, as if this were to be his name for
ever, and this his memorial to all generations: as "he that
rides upon the heavens," by his name "Jah," is the "Father
of the fatherless, and the Judge of the widows" (Psalm 118:
4, 5). Some make his name *Christos* to have an allusion to
Chrestos, which signifies kind, and gentle, and gracious.
Christ rides prosperously "because of meekness" (Psalm
95: 4).

Now it is the character of all the saints that they follow
the Lamb (Rev. 14:4). As a lamb they follow him in his
meekness, and are therefore so often called "the sheep of
Christ." This is that part of his copy which he expressly

calls us to write after: "Learn of me, for I am meek and lowly in heart" (Matt. 21: 29). If the master be mild, it ill becomes the servant to be froward. The apostle is speaking of Christ's meekness under his sufferings when he says that "he left us an example, and we should follow his steps" (1 Pet. 2: 21).

Let us observe particularly the meekness of our Lord Jesus, both towards his Father, and towards his friends, and towards his foes: in each of which he is an example to us.

(1) *He was very meek toward God his Father,* cheerfully submitting to his whole will, and standing complete in it. In his commanding will, "Lo I come," says he, "I delight to do thy will"; though it enjoined him a very hard piece of service, yet it was his "meat and drink" (John 4:34), and "he always did those things that pleased his Father" (John 8:29). So likewise in his disposing will, he acquiesced from first to last. When he was entering on that sharp encounter, though sense startled at it, and said "Father, if it be possible, let the cup pass from me"; yet he soon submitted with a great deal of meekness. "Not as I will, but as thou wilt," he said (Matt. 26: 39, 42). Though it was a very bitter cup, yet his Father put it into his hand, and therefore he drank it without any struggle or reluctance, when it came to the point, reasoning himself from that topic into this compliance: "The cup that my Father hath given me, shall I not drink it? (John 18: 11). And it comes in there as a reason why he would not have a sword drawn in his defence.

(2) *He was very meek towards his friends* that loved and followed him. With what remarkable instances of mildness, and gentleness, and tenderness, did he train up his disciples. Though from first to last he was "a man of sorrows, and acquainted with grief," and where the nature is corrupt such men are apt to be peevish and froward with

those about them, he was meek and calm, as we may see in
at least two ways.

First, in his bearing with the weaknesses and infirmities
of his friends. After they had been long under the inspec-
tion and influence of such a teacher, and had all the advantages that men could have for getting acquainted with the
things of God, how weak and defective they were, after all,
in knowledge, and gifts, and graces. How ignorant and for-
getful they were! How slow of heart to understand and believe! And what blunders they made! Dull scholars it would
seem they were, and never proficient. But their hearts were
upright with him, and so he did not cast them off nor turn
them out of his school. Rather he made the best of them,
rectified their mistakes, instructed them in their duty, and
the doctrine they were to preach, by "precept upon precept,"
and "line upon line." He taught them as they were able to
bear it, as one that considered their frame and could have
compassion on the "ignorant," and on them that are "out of
the way" (Heb. 5:2). As long as he was with them, so long
he suffered them (Mark 9: 19). This, as it is a great encouragement to Christian learners, so it is a great example
to Christian teachers.

Second, in his forgiving and passing by their unkindnesses
and disrespects to himself. He was not extreme to mark
what they did amiss of this kind. When they murmured at
the cost that was bestowed upon him, and called it waste,
and had indignation at it, he did not resent it as he might
have done, nor seem to observe how much what they said
reflected upon him; nor did he condemn them any other way
than by commending the woman (Matt. 26: 8, 11). When
Peter and James and John, the first three of his disciples,
were with him in the garden, and very unseasonably slept
while he was in his agony praying, so little concerned did
they seem to be for him, and such a grievous slight did they

put upon him; yet observe, how meekly he spoke to them saying, "Could ye not watch with me one hour?" And when they had not a word to say for themselves, so inexcusable was their fault, he had something to say for them, and instead of accusing them, he apologizes for them, "The spirit indeed is willing, but the flesh is weak" (Matt. 26: 40, 41). When Peter had denied him, and had cursed and sworn he did not know him, than which (besides the falsehood and perfidiousness of it) nothing could be more unkind, with what meekness did he bear it! It is not said the Lord turned and frowned upon Peter, though he deserved to be frowned into hell, but it is said that "the Lord turned and looked upon Peter" (Luke 22: 61), and that look recovered him into the way to heaven. It was a kind look and not an angry one. Some days after, when Christ and Peter met in Galilee, and had dined together as a token of reconciliation, and some discourse passed between them, not a word was said of this matter. Christ did not upbraid him with his fault, he did not chide him for it, nor did there appear any other fruit of the falling out of these lovers, but only the renewing of their love with greater endearments (John 21: 15-17), which teaches us to forgive and forget the unkindness of those that are for the main our true friends. If any occasion of difference occur, we should turn it into an occasion of confirming our love to them, as the apostle expresses it in 2 Corinthians 2: 8.

(3) *He was very meek toward his enemies* who hated and persecuted him. The whole story of his life is filled with instances of invincible meekness. While he "endured the contradiction of sinners against himself," which was a constant jar, he had a perpetual serenity and harmony within himself, and was never in the least discomposed by it. When his preaching and miracles were scoffed at and reproached, and he himself represented under the

blackest characters, not only as the drunkard's companion, but as the devil's confederate, with what a wonderful calmness did he bear it! How mildly did he answer, with reason and tenderness, when he could have replied in thunder and lightning! How well satisfied, under all such invidious reflections, was he with this: "Wisdom is however justified of all her children!" (Matt. 11: 19). When some of his disciples would have had fire from heaven upon those rude people that refused him entertainment in their town, he was so far from complying with the suggestion that he rebuked it: "Ye know not what manner of spirit ye are of" (Luke 9: 55). "This persuasion cometh not of him that calleth you" (Gal. 5: 8). The design of Christ and of his holy religion is to shape men into a mild and merciful temper, and to make them sensibly tender of the lives and comforts even of their worst enemies. Christianity was intended to revive humanity, and to make those men, who had made themselves beasts. But our Lord Jesus did in a more special manner evidence his meekness when he was in his last sufferings, that awful scene. Though he was the most innocent and the most excellent person that ever was, who by the doctrine he had preached and the miracles he had wrought had richly deserved all the honors and respects that the world could pay him, and infinitely more, and though the injuries he received were ingeniously and industriously contrived to the highest degree of affront and provocation, yet he bore all with an undisturbed meekness, and with that shield quenched all the fiery darts which his malicious enemies shot at him.

His meekness towards his enemies appeared first, in what he said to them. In the midst of all the indignities they offered him, he uttered not one angry word: "When he was reviled, he reviled not again" (1 Pet. 2:23). When he was buffeted and spit upon, and abused, he took it all patiently. One would wonder at the gracious words which even then proceeded out of his mouth. Witness that mild reply to him that smote him: "If I have spoken evil, bear witness of the evil; but if well, why smitest thou me?" (John 18: 23).

His meekness towards his enemies appeared second, in what he said to God for them: "Father, forgive them" (Matt. 5: 44). He gave an example to his own rule, "Pray for them which despitefully use you." Though he was then deeply engaged in the most solemn transaction that ever passed between heaven and earth; though he had so much to do with God for himself and his friends, yet he did not forget to put up this prayer for his enemies. The mercy he begged of God for them was the greatest mercy (that which he was then dying to purchase and procure): the pardon of their sins. He said not only, Father, spare them, or reprieve them, but "Father, forgive them." The excuse he pleaded for them was the best their crime was capable of: "They know not what they do." They did it ignorantly (1 Cor. 2:8; 1 Tim. 1:13).

Now in all these things our Master has left us an example. What is the practice of religion but the imitation of God endeavored by us? And what the principle of it, but the image of God renewed in us? We are bid to be followers of God, as dear children. But this sets the copy we are to write after at a mighty distance, for God is in heaven and we are upon earth. Therefore in the Lord Jesus Christ, God incarnate, God in our nature, the copy is brought among us, and the transcribing of it, in some measure, appears more practicable. "He that hath seen me hath seen the Father" says Christ (John 14:9), and so he that imitates Christ imitates the Father. The religion which our Lord Jesus came into the world to establish is calculated for the peace and order of the world, is designed to recover the lapsed souls of men from their degenerate state, and to sweeten their spirits and tem-

per, and so to befriend human society and to make it some
way conformable to the blessed society above. Our Lord Jesus not only gave such precepts as were wonderfully fitted to
this great end, but he recommended them to the world by the
loveliness and amiableness of his own example. Are we not
called Christians from Christ whom we call Master and
Lord, and shall we not endeavor to accommodate ourselves
to him? We profess to rejoice in him as our forerunner:
shall we not then run after him? To what purpose were we
listed under his banner but that we might follow him as our
leader? We have all of us reason to say that Jesus Christ is
very meek or else we, who have provoked him so much and
so often, would have been in hell long ago. We owe it to his
meekness, to whom all judgment is committed, that we have
not ere this been carried away with a swift destruction and
dealt with according to the desert of our sins, which, if
duly considered, one would think should tend greatly to the
softening of us. The apostle fetches an argument from that
kindness and love to us which we ourselves have experienced,
who were foolish and disobedient, to persuade us to "be
gentle and to show all meekness" (Tit. 3: 2-4); and he beseeches the Corinthians by "the meekness and gentleness of
Christ" as a thing very winning, and of dear and precious account (2 Cor. 10: 1). "Let the same mind therefore be in
us," not only which was, but which, as we find to our comfort, "still is, in Christ Jesus" (Phil. 2: 5). That we may not
forfeit our interest in his meekness, let us tread in the steps of
it; and as ever we hoped to be like him in glory hereafter, let
us study to be like him in grace, in this grace now. It is a
certain rule, by which we must all be tried shortly, "that if
any man hath not the Spirit of Christ" (that is, if he be not
spirited, in some measure, as Christ was spirited), "he is none
of his" (Rom. 8:9). And if we be not owned as his, we are
undone forever.

III. *Some Particular Instances wherein the Exercise of Meekness is in a Special Manner Required*

The rule is general: we must "show all meekness." It will be of use to observe some special cases to which the Scripture applies this general rule.

a. *We must give reproofs with meekness.* This is the apostle's direction: "If a man be overtaken in a fault" (that is, if he be surprised by a temptation and overcome, as the best may be if God leave them to themselves), "ye which are spiritual, restore such a one in the spirit of meekness" (Gal. 6:1). By the spiritual man, to whom he gives this rule, he means not ministers only, as if none were spiritual but they, though they perhaps are chiefly intended because they are "reprovers in the gate" (Isa. 29:21), that is, reprovers by office, but doubtless this is a rule to private Christians. All who have opportunity must reprove, and all who reprove must do it with meekness. Ye that are spiritual, if you would approve yourselves so indeed, actuated by the Holy Spirit and minding the things of the Spirit, be careful in this matter. Especially let those who are Christians of the highest form, who excel in grace and holiness and the best gifts (such are called spiritual in distinction from the babes in Christ: 1 Cor. 3: 1), let them look upon themselves as obliged in a more particular manner to help others. For where God gives five talents, he expects the improvement of five: the strong must "bear the infirmities of the weak" (Rom. 15:1). Do you therefore "restore such a one," *Katartizete* — "set him in joint again." The setting of a dislocated or a broken joint is, for the present, painful to the patient, but it must be done, and it is in order to the making of "broken bones to rejoice." Now this ye must do with the spirit of meekness, with all the candor and gentleness and convincing evidences of love and kindness that can be. The three qualifications of a good surgeon are requisite in a reprover: he should have an

eagle's eye, a lion's heart, and a lady's hand; in short, he
should be endued with wisdom, and courage, and meekness.
Though sometimes it is needful to reprove with warmth, yet
we must never reprove with wrath "for the wrath of man
worketh not the righteousness of God" (James 1:20). There
is an observable difference, but no contradiction, between the
directions Paul gives to Timothy and those he gives to Titus
in this matter. To Titus he writes to "reprove sharply" (Tit.
1:13) and to rebuke "with all authority" (Tit. 2: 15). To
Timothy he writes "not to strive," but "to be gentle" (2 Tim.
2: 24), to reprove "with all long-suffering" (2 Tim. 4:2).
The reason for this difference may be the difference in the
people with whom they were dealing. Timothy was among
the Ephesians, a tractable complaisant people who would be
easily managed, and with them he must always deal gently.
Titus was among the Cretans, who were head-strong and
rough-hewn and not to be wrought upon but by sharper
methods. Thus, in reproving, a difference must be made: on
some we must have compassion, others we must save with
fear, but never with anger, plucking them out of the fire
(Jude 23). Or the reason for the difference may be the difference in Timothy and Titus. "Titus was a man of very
soft and mild temper, and he had need of a spur to quicken
him to a needful acrimony in his reproofs: but Timothy was
a man of a more warm and sanguine temper, and he had
need of a bridle to keep him from an intemperate heat in his
reproofs," says Gregory, one of the ancients. Those who are
naturally keen and fervent should double their guard upon
their own spirits when they are reproving that they may do
it with all meekness. Christ's ministers must be careful, while
they display God's wrath, to conceal their own. They must
be very jealous over themselves lest sinful anger shelter itself under the cloak of zeal against sin. When reproving
(whoever be the reprover) degenerates into railing and re-

viling and opprobrious language, how can we expect the desired success? It may provoke to contention, and every evil work, but it will never provoke to love, and to good works. The work of heaven is not likely to be done by a tongue set on fire of hell. Has Christ need of madmen? or will you talk deceitfully and passionately for him? A potion given too hot scalds the patient, and does more harm than good; and so many a reproof, good for the matter of it, has been spoiled by an irregular management. Meekness hides the lancet, gilds the pill, and makes it passable; meekness dips the nail in oil, and then it drives the better. Twice we find Jonathan reproving his father for his rage against David. Once he did it with meekness and it succeeded well: "Let not the king sin against his servant" (1 Sam. 19: 4, 5), and it is said that "Saul hearkened to him" (1 Sam: 19: 6). But another time his spirit was provoked, and he did it with anger: "Wherefore shall he be slain?" (1 Sam. 20: 32); and the issue of it was ill. Saul was not only impatient of the reproof, but enraged at the reprover, and cast a javelin at him. Reproofs are then likely to answer the intention when they manifestly evidence the good will of the reprover, and are made up of soft words and hard arguments. This is to restore with the spirit of meekness, and there is a good reason added, considering thyself: *ille hodie, ego cras* — he may fall today, I may tomorrow. Those who think they stand fast know not how soon they may be shaken and overthrown, and, therefore, we must treat those that are overtaken in a fault with the same tenderness and compassion that we would wish to find if it were our own case.

b. *We must receive reproofs with meekness.* If we do that which deserves rebuke, and we meet with those who are so just and kind as to give us a rebuke, we must be quiet under it, not quarreling with the reprover, nor objecting against the reproof, nor fretting that we are touched in a

sore place; but submit to it, and lay our souls under the conviction of it. If reproofs be physic, it becomes us to be
patient. "Let the righteous smite me, it shall be a kindness
and an excellent oil," healing to the wounds of sin, and making the face to shine; and let us never reckon that it "breaks
the head" if it do but help to "break the heart." Meekness suffers the word of admonition, and takes it patiently and thankfully, not only from the hand of God who sends it, but from
the hand of our friend who brings it. We must not be like
the reprobate Sodomites (Gen. 19:9) or that pert Hebrew
(Exod. 2:14) who flew in the face of their reprovers (though
really they were the best friends they had) with, "Who made
thee a judge?" We must be like David who, when Abigail so
prudently slowed the wheels of his passion, not only blest
God who sent her, and blest her advice, but blest her (1 Sam.
25: 32, 33 and 35). He not only "hearkened to her voice,
but accepted her person." Though perhaps the reprover supposes the fault greater than it really was, and though the reproof be not given with all the prudence in the world, yet
meekness will teach us to accept it quietly and to make the
best use we can of it. Even if we be altogether innocent of that
which we are reproved for, yet the meekness of wisdom
would teach us to apply the reproof to some other fault which
our own consciences convict us of; we would not quarrel with
a real intended kindness, though not done with ceremony,
and though in some circumstances mistaken or misplaced.

You who are in inferior relations, children, servants, scholars, must with all meekness and submission receive the reproofs of your parents, masters, and teachers: their age supposes them to have more understanding than you; however,
their place gives them an authority over you, to which you
are to pay a deference, and in which you are to acquiesce —
else farewell all order and peace in societies. The angel rebuked Hagar for flying from her mistress, though she dealt

hardly with her, and obliged her to return and submit herself "under her hands" (Gen. 16: 6, 9). "If the spirit of any ruler rise up against thee," and thou be chidden for a fault, "leave not thy place," as an inferior, "for yielding pacifies great offences done" and prevents the like (Eccl. 19: 4). "If thou hast thought evil, lay thine hand upon thy mouth" to keep that evil thought from breaking out in any undue and unbecoming language (Prov. 30: 32). Reproofs are then likely to do us good when we meekly submit to them. Then are they as an "ear-ring of gold," and an "ornament of fine gold" when an obedient ear is given to a wise reprover (Prov. 25: 12). Nay, even superiors are to receive reproofs from their inferiors with meekness, as they would any other token of kindness and good will. Naaman, when he turned away from the prophet in a rage, yet hearkened to the reproof his own servants gave him, and was overruled by the reason of it (2 Kings 5: 11-14). This was no more a disparagement to him than it was to receive instruction from his wife's maid to "whom to go for a cure of his leprosy" (2 Kings 5: 2, 3). Meekness teaches us when a just reproof is given to regard not so much who speaks as what is spoken.

c. *We must instruct gainsayers with meekness* (2 Tim. 2:24, 25). It is prescribed to ministers that they must not strive but be "gentle to all men, in meekness instructing those that oppose themselves." They serve the Prince of Peace, they preach the gospel of peace, they are the ambassadors of peace, and therefore must be sure to keep the peace. The apostles, those prime-ministers of state in Christ's kingdom, were not military men, or men of strife and noise, but fishermen who followed their employment with quietness and silence. It is highly necessary that the guides of the church be strict governors of their own passions. "Learn of me for I am meek and lowly," says Christ (Matt. 11: 29); and therefore I am fit to teach you. We must contend earnestly, but not angrily and passionately, no not "for the faith once delivered to the saints" (Jude 3). When we have ever so great an assurance that it is the cause of truth we are pleading, yet we must so manage our defence of it against those who gainsay, as to make it appear that it is not the confusion of the erroneous, but the confutation of the error, that we intend. This meekness would teach us not to pre-judge a cause, nor to condemn an adversary unheard, but calmly to state matters in difference, as knowing that a truth well opened is half confirmed. It would teach us not to aggravate matters in dispute, nor to father upon an adversary all the absurd consequences which we think may be inferred from his opinion: it would teach us to judge charitably of those who differ from us and to forbear all personal reflections in arguing with them. God's cause needs not the patronage of our sinful hearts and passions, which not only shatter the peace, but often give a mighty shock even to the truth itself for which we plead. Meekness would prevent and cure that bigotry which has been so long the bane of the church, and contribute a great deal towards the advancement of that happy state in which, notwithstanding little differences of apprehension and opinion, "The Lord shall be one, and his name one." Public reformations are carried on with most credit and comfort, and are most likely to settle our lasting foundations, when meekness sits at the stern and guides the emotions of them. When Christ was purging the temple, though he was therein actuated by a zeal for God's house that even ate him up, yet he did it with meekness and prudence, which appeared in this instance: when he drove out the sheep and oxen, which would easily be caught again, he said to them who sold doves, "Take these things hence" (John 2: 16). He did not let loose the doves, and send them flying, for that would have been to the loss and prejudice of the owners. Angry, noisy, bitter arguings ill become the asserters of the truth which is great and will prevail without all that ado. It was a very froward and perverse generation our Lord Jesus lived in, and yet it is said, "He shall not strive, nor cry, neither shall any man hear his voice in the street" (Matt. 12: 19). Though our Lord Jesus could have broken them as easily as a bruised reed, and extinguish them as soon as one could quench the wick of a candle newly lighted, yet he will not do it till the day comes when he shall "bring forth judgment unto victory." Moses dealt with a very obstinate and stiff-necked people, and yet "my doctrine shall drop as the dew, and distil as the small rain," he said (Deut. 32: 2). It was not the wind, nor the earthquake, nor the fire, that brought Elijah into temper (for the Lord was not in them), but the still small voice did it; when he heard that he "wrapt his face in his mantle" (1 Kings 19: 11-13). In dealing with gainsayers a spirit of meekness will teach us to consider their temper, education, custom, the power of prejudice they labor under, the influence of others upon them, and to make allowances accordingly and not to call, as passionate contenders are apt to do, every false step an apostasy, every error a mistake; nay, every misconstrued, misplaced word a heresy, and every misdemeanor no less than treason and rebellion. Such methods of proceeding are more likely to irritate and harden than to convince and reduce gainsayers. I have heard it observed long since "that the scourge of the tongue has driven many out of the temple, but never drove any into it."

d. *We must make profession of the hope that is in us with meekness.* "Be ready always to give answer," to make your *defence* or *apology,* as the word is in the original, whether judicially or extrajudicially, as there is occasion, "to every man that asks you a reason, or an account of the hope that is in you," that is, of the hope you profess, which you hope to be saved by, with "meekness and fear" (1 Pet. 3: 15). Observe, it is consistent with Christian quietness to appear in the defence of truth and to avow our Christian profession when at any time we are duly called to it. That is not meekness but base cowardice that tamely betrays and delivers up any of Christ's truths or institutions by silence, as if we were ashamed or afraid to confess our Master. But the office of meekness at such a time is to direct us how and in what manner to bear our testimony, not with pride and passion, but with humility and mildness. Those who would successfully confess the truth must first learn to deny themselves: and we must give an account of our hope with a holy fear of missing it in such a critical juncture. When we give a reason for our religion, we must not boast of ourselves or of our own attainments, nor reflect contempt and wrath upon our persecutors, but remember that the *present truth* (as it is called in 2 Pet. 1: 12), the truth which is now to be asserted, is the same with "the word of Christ's patience" (Rev. 3: 10), that is, the word which must be patiently suffered for, according to the example of him, who with invincible meekness, before Pontius Pilate, "witnessed a good confession" (1 Tim. 6: 13). A great abasement and diffidence of ourselves may very well consist with a firm assurance of the truth and a profound veneration for it.

In lesser things, wherein wise and good men are not all of a mind, meekness teaches us not to be too confident that we are in the right, nor to censure and condemn those that differ from us, as if we were the people, and wisdom should die with us. Meekness teaches us to walk quietly according to the light that God has given us, and charitably to believe that others do so too, waiting till God shall reveal either this to them (Phil. 3: 15) or that to us. Let it in such cases suffice to vindicate ourselves, which every man has a right to do, without a magisterial sentencing of others. Why should, we be many masters when we are all offenders (Jam. 3: 1, 2), and the bar is our place, not the bench? Meekness will likewise teach us to manage a singular opinion wherein we differ from others with all possible deference to them, and suspicion of ourselves; not resenting it as affront to be contradicted, but taking it as a kindness to be better informed. Nor must we be angry that our hope is inquired into: even such a trial of it, if we approve ourselves well in it, may be "found to praise and honor and glory" to which our meekness will very much contribute, as it puts a luster upon, and a convincing power into, the testimony we bear. We then walk worthy of the "vocation wherein we are called, when we walk in all lowliness and meekness" (Eph. 4: 1, 2).

e. *We must bear reproaches with meekness.* Reproach is a branch of that persecution which all that will live godly in Christ Jesus must count upon; and we must submit to it, behaving ourselves quietly, and with a due decorum, not only when princes sit and speak against us, but even when the abjects gather themselves together against us, and we become the song of the drunkards. Sometimes we find it easier to keep calm in a solemn and expected engagement than in a sudden skirmish or a hasty encounter; and therefore, even against those slight attacks, it is requisite that meekness be set upon the guard. If we be nick-named and slandered, and have all manner of evil said against us falsely, our rule is not to be disturbed at it, nor "to render railing for railing" (1 Pet. 3: 9), though we may, as we have opportunity, with meekness, deny the charge. So Hannah did when Eli too hastily censured her for a drunkard: "No, my lord, I have drunk neither wine nor strong drink" (1 Sam. 1: 15). Yet, when that is done, we must, without meditating any revenge, quietly commit our cause to God who will, sooner or later, clear up our "innocency as the light" (Psalm 37: 5, 6). Therefore "fret not thyself, but wait patiently . . . . . cease

from anger, and forsake wrath" (Psalm 37:7, 8). We do
but gratify our great adversary, and do his work for him,
when we suffer the peace and serenity of our minds to be
broken in upon by the reproaches of the world. For me to
disquiet myself and put myself into a passion because another abuses me, is as if I should scratch up the skin of
my face to fetch off the dirt which my adversary throws
in it. When reproaches provoke our passions, which put us
upon rendering bitterness for bitterness, we thereby lose the
comfort, and forfeit the honor and reward which the divine
promise has annexed to the reproach of Christ; and shall
we suffer so many things in vain? We likewise thereby give
occasion to those who had spoken evil of us falsely, to speak
evil of us truly; and perhaps our religion suffers more by
our impatience under the reproach than by the reproach
itself. What have we the law and pattern and promise of
Christ for but to calm our spirit under reproaches for well-
doing? Truly those can bear but a little for Christ who cannot bear a hard or an unkind word for him. If we either
faint or fret in such a day of adversity, it is a sign our
strength is small indeed. May it not satisfy us that by our
meekness and quietness under reproaches we engage God
for us, who has promised that he will "with righteousness
judge the poor," the poor in spirit, "and will reprove with
equity for the meek of the earth" (Isa. 11: 4). He that
has bid us "to open our mouths for the dumb" (Prov. 31:8)
will not himself be silent. And shall we not learn at last,
instead of fretting and being exceeding angry, to "rejoice"
and be "exceeding glad" (Matt. 5: 11, 12) when we suffer
thus for righteousness sake? May we not put such reproaches as pearls in our crown, and be assured that they
will pass well in the account another day when there will
be an advantageous resurrection of names as well as bodies?
In the prospect of this day we have reason to rejoice "that

we are counted worthy to suffer shame for his name" (Acts 5: 41), that we are honored to be dishonored for him who for our sakes endured the cross and despised the shame. It is one of the laws of meekness, *Spernere se spernit* — "to despise being despised."

IV. Some Good Principles or Considerations which Tend to Make us Meek and Quiet

In order to govern the soul well the judgment must be furnished with proper dictates; else it will never be able to keep the peace in the affections. The motions of the soul are then likely to be even, and regular, and constant, when we have fixed to ourselves good principles which we are governed by, and act under the influence of. There are some carnal corrupt principles which angry froward people are guided by, such as this: "Forgiving one injury invites another"; whereas it often qualifies an adversary, or if otherwise, the forgiving of one offence will enable us to bear the next the more easily. Or this: "We must have satisfaction given us for every wrong done us"; whereas, if we have not satisfaction for it, yet if it be not our own fault, we may have satisfaction under it, and that is as good. And this: "There is no living in the world without huffing and hectoring, and frightening people; *Oderint dum metuant* — let them hate, provided they fear"; whereas, to live continually in that element is to live in a hell upon earth; mutual indignation and mutual fear perhaps contributing to the torment of devils and damned spirits. In opposition to these and similar bad principles we should treasure these few good truths chosen out of many which might be mentioned and make use of them as there is occasion.

a. *That he has the sweetest and surest peace who is the most master of his own passions.* The comfort that a man has in governing himself is much greater than he could

have in having people serve him and nations bow down
to him. It is certain that the worst enemies we have, if ever
they break loose and get head, are in our own bosoms. Enemies without threaten only the evil of pain; they can but
kill the body and no great hurt in that to a child of God, if
they do not provoke the enemies within, our own irregular
passions, which, if they be not kept under, plunge us in the
evil of sin, and that is a much greater evil. An invasion
from abroad does not so much disturb the peace of a kingdom as an insurrection at home; and therefore it concerns
us to double our guard, where our danger is greatest, and
above all keepings to keep our hearts that no passion be allowed to stir, without a good reason be given for it, and a
good use made of it. And then, if we be "troubled on every
side, yet not distressed; perplexed, yet not in despair" (2
Cor. 4: 8, 9), offended by our fellow-servants, but not
offending our master; reproached by our neighbors, but not
by our own consciences; that is like Zion's peace, "peace
within the walls" (Psalm 122:7). We have no need to
pray as one did, *Libera me a malo isto homine me-ipso* —
"Lord, deliver me from that ill man, mine own self," and
then I am safe enough. The "lusts that war in our members" (James 4: 1) are the "enemies that war against our
souls" (1 Pet. 2:11). If this war be brought to a good issue,
and those enemies suppressed, whatsoever other disturbances
are given, peace is in the soul "with grace and mercy from God,
and from the Lord Jesus." Nehemiah was aware of this as
the design of his enemies when they hired a pretended prophet to give an alarm, and to advise him meanly to shift for
himself: it was, says Nehemiah, "that I should be afraid, and
do so, and sin" (Neh. 6: 13). Whatever we lose, we should
not lose our peace, if we do but keep our integrity; therefore,
instead of being solicitous to subdue our enemies that lay
siege to us, let us double our watch against the traitors with-

in the garrison, from whom, especially, our danger is. Since we cannot prevent the shooting of the fiery darts, let us have our shield ready wherewith to quench them. If we would not hurt ourselves, blessed be God, no enemy in the world can hurt us. Let us but keep the peace within, by the governing of our passions; and then, whatever assaults may be made upon us, we may therein, with the daughter of Zion, despise them, and laugh them to scorn, and shake our head at them (Isa. 37:22). Let us believe that in hurrying and disquieting times our strength is to sit still, in a holy quietness and composure of mind: "This is the rest wherewith you may cause the weary to rest; and this is the refreshing;" and it is enough (Isa. 28: 12).

b. *That in many things we all offend.* This truth we have (James 3:2), and it comes in as a reason why we must not be many masters (verse 1). It would help to subdue and moderate our anger at the offences of others, if we would but consider two things.

First, that it is incident to human nature to offend. While we are in this world we must not expect to converse with angels, or the spirits of just men made perfect. No, we are obliged to have communication with creatures who are foolish and corrupt, peevish and provoking, and who are all subject to like passions; such as these we must live among, else must we needs go out of the world. And have we not reason then to count upon something or other uneasy and displeasing in all relations and conversations? The best men have their roughnesses and unevennesses in this imperfect state; those who are savingly enlightened, yet knowing but in part, have their blind side. The harmony, even of the communion of saints, will sometimes be disturbed with jarring strings. Why then should we be surprised into passion and disquiet when that which gives us the disturbance is no more than what we looked for? Instead of being angry, we should think with ourselves thus: Alas! what could I expect but provocation from corrupt and fallen man? Among such foolish creatures as we are, it must needs be that offences will come; and why should not I have my share of those offences? The God of heaven gives this as a reason of his patience towards a provoking world that it is in their nature to be provoking: "I will not again curse the ground any more for man's sake, for the imagination of man's heart is evil from his youth" (Gen. 8: 21), and therefore better is not to be expected from him. And upon this account he had compassion on Israel, "For he remembered that they were but flesh" (Psalm 78:39); not only frail creatures, but sinful, and prone to backslide. "Do men gather grapes of thorns? I knew that thou wouldst deal treacherously, for thou wast called a transgressor from the womb" (Isa. 48: 8). And should not we, much more, be governed by the same consideration? "If thou seest the violent perverting of judgment and justice in a province," remember what a provoking creature sinful man is, and then thou wilt not "marvel at the matter" (Eccl. 5: 8). The consideration of the common infirmity and corruption of mankind should be made use of, not to excuse our own faults to ourselves, which does but take off the edge of our repentance, and is the poor subterfuge of a deceived heart; but to excuse the faults of others, and so take off the edge of our passion and displeasure, and preserve the meekness and quietness of our spirits.

Second, that it is incident to ourselves, among the rest, to offend. The apostle there puts himself into the number, saying, "We all offend." We offend God; if we say we do not, we deceive ourselves, and yet he bears with us from day to day, and is not extreme to mark what we do amiss, though our debts to him are talents, our brethren's to us but pence. Think then, if God should be as angry with me for every provocation as I am with those about me what would become of me? They are careless in their observance, and perhaps wilful in their offence, and am not I so to God? Yea, am not I a thousand times worse? Job said, when his servants were provoking, and he was tempted to be harsh with them, "What then shall I do, when God riseth up? and when he visiteth, what shall I answer him?" (Job 31: 13, 14).

And are we not enough likewise to offend our brethren? Either we have offended, or may offend; so that we have need that others should bear with us, and why should we not bear with them. *Hanc veniam petimusque damusque vicissim* — "Let us seek and grant pardon alternately." Our rule is: "What we would that men should do to us when we offend them, the same we should do to them when they offend us," for "this is the law and the prophets" (Matt. 7: 12). Solomon appeals to our consciences herein (Eccl. 7: 22). For "oftentimes also thine own heart" (which is instead of a thousand witnesses) "knoweth that thou thyself likewise hath cursed others." The penitent remembrance of former guilt would greatly help to curb the passionate resentment of present trouble. When the undutiful rebellious son (in a story that I once read) dragged his father by the hair of the head to the house door, it appeased the anger of the old man to remember that just so far he had dragged his father; and it seems to have silenced Adonibezek that he was now treated no otherwise than he had treated others (Judg. 1: 7).

c. *That men are God's hand, as it is said:* "From men which are thy hand, O Lord," (Psalm 17: 14), or rather, *tools* in thy hand (verse 13), which are thy *sword*. We must abide by this principle that whatever it is that crosses us, or is displeasing to us at any time, God has an overruling hand in it. David was governed by this principle when he bore Shimri's spiteful reproaches with such invincible patience: "So let him curse, because the Lord hath said unto him, Curse David" (2 Sam. 16: 10); "Let him alone, for the Lord hath bidden him" (2 Sam. 16: 11). This consideration will not only silence our murmurings against God, the author, but all our quarellings with men, the instruments of our trouble and vexation. Men's reproaches are God's rebukes, and whoever he be that affronts me I must see and say that therein my Father corrects me. This quieted the spirit of Job, in reference to the injuries of the Chaldeans and Sabeans, though he dwelt as a "king in the army" (Job 29: 25), and his power and interest seem to have been sustained when those intruders first made that inroad upon him, and so he could not but see his help in the gate; yet we find him not meditating any revenge, but calming the disturbances of his own soul with the consideration of God's sovereign disposal, overlooking all the instruments of his trouble, thoughts of which would but have mingled anger (the more disquieting passion) with his sorrow. This therefore suffices to still the storm: "The Lord gave, and the Lord hath taken away, blessed be the name of the Lord" (Job 1: 21). When his brethren stood aloof from him, his kindred and his friends looked scornfully upon him, as an alien, and instead of oil, poured vinegar into his wounds so that his "eye continued in this provocation," yet even in that part of his trouble he owns the hand of God: "He hath put my brethren far from me" (Job 19: 13). It is a very quieting truth (the Lord help us to mix faith with it) that every creature is that to us, and no more, that God makes it to be; and, that while many seek the ruler's favor, and more perhaps fear the ruler's displeasure, "every man's judgment proceedeth from the Lord." Would we but more closely observe, and readily own, the hand of God in that which disquiets and provokes us, surely, though we regard not man, yet if we had any fear of God before our eyes, that would reconcile us better to it, and suppress all intemperate and undue resentments. In murmuring at the stone, we reflect upon the hand that throws it, and lay ourselves under the woe pronounced against him "that strives with his Maker" (Isa. 45: 9). We know it is interpreted as taking up arms against the king if we take up arms against any that are commissioned by him.

d. *That there is no provocation given us* at any time but, if it be skillfully and graciously improved, there is good to be gotten by it. If we have but that wisdom of the prudent which is "to understand his way," and all the advantages and opportunities of it, doubtless we may, quite contrary to the intention of those who trespass against us, gain some spiritual, that is, some real, benefit to our souls by the injuries and offences that are done to us, for even these are made to "work together for good to them that love God." This is a holy and happy way of opposing our adversaries, and resisting evil. It is an ill weed indeed out of which the spiritual bee cannot extract something profitable and for its purpose. Whatever lion roars against us, let us but go in the strength and spirit of the Lord, as Samson did, and we may not only rend it as a kid, so that it shall do us no real harm, but we may withal get "meat out of the eater, and sweetness out of the strong." As it turns to the unspeakable prejudice of many that they look upon reproofs as reproaches, and treat them accordingly with anger and displeasure, so it would turn to our unspeakable advantage if we could but learn to call reproaches reproofs, and make use of them as such for our conviction and humiliation; and thus the reproach of Christ may become true riches to us, and greater than the treasures of Egypt.

We are told of an abscess that was cured with the thrust of an enemy's sword; and of one that was happily converted from drunkenness by being called, in reproach, "a tippler."

It is very possible that we may be enlightened, or humbled, or reformed, may be brought nearer to God, or weaned from the world, may be furnished with matter for repentance, or prayer, or praise, by the injuries that are done us, and may be much furthered in our way to heaven by that which was intended for an affront or provocation. This principle would put another aspect upon injuries and unkindnesses, and would quite alter the property of them, and teach us to call them by another name. Whatever the subordinate instrument intended, it is likely "he meant not so, neither did his heart think so" (Isa. 10:7), but God designed it, as our other afflictions, to yield the "peaceable fruit of righteousness; so that instead of being angry at the man that meant us ill, we should rather be thankful to the God that intended us good, and study to answer his intention. This kept Joseph in that good temper towards his brethren, though he had occasion enough to quarrel with them: "You thought evil against me, but God meant it unto good" (Gen. 50: 20). This satisfied Paul, in reference to the thorn in the flesh, that is, the calumnies and oppositions of the false apostles, which touched him more sensibly than all the efforts of persecuting rage; that it was intended to hide pride from him "lest he should be exalted above measure, with the abundance of revelations" (2 Cor. 12: 7). There seems to be an instance of that good effect it had upon him immediately upon the mention of it, for within a few lines after he lets fall that humble word, "I am nothing" (2 Cor. 12: 11). We should be apt to think too highly of ourselves, and too kindly of the world, if we did not meet with some injuries and contempts, by which we are taught to cease from man. Did we but more carefully study the improvement of an injury, we should not be so apt to desire the revenge of it.

e. *That what is said and done in haste* is likely to be matter for deliberate repentance. We find David often remembering with regret what he said in his haste, particularly one angry word he had said in the day of his distress and trouble, which seemed to reflect upon Samuel, and indeed upon all that had given him any encouragement to hope for the kingdom: "I said in my haste, all men are liars" (Psalm 116: 11); and this hasty word was a grief to him long after. "He that hasteth with his feet, sinneth" (Prov. 19: 2). When a man is transported by passion into any impropriety, we commonly qualify it with this statement, "he is a little hasty," as if there were no harm in that. But we see there is harm in it. He that is in haste may contract much guilt in a little time. What we say or do unadvisedly when we are hot, we must unsay or undo again when we are cool, or do worse. Now who would wilfully do that which sooner or later he must repent of? A heathen that was tempted to a chargeable sin could resist the temptation with this consideration, "that he would not buy repentance so dear." Is repentance such a pleasant work that we should so industriously treasure up unto ourselves wrath against the day of wrath, either the day of God's wrath against us, or our own wrath against ourselves? You little think what a torrent of self-affliction you let in when you let the reins loose to an immoderate ungoverned passion. You are angry at others, and reproach them, and call them hard names, and are ready to abhor them, and to revenge yourselves upon them; and your corrupt nature takes a strange kind of pleasure in this; but do you know that all this will at last rebound in your own faces, and return into your own bosoms? Either here, or in a worse place, you must repent of all this; that is, you must turn all these passions upon yourselves, you must be angry at yourselves, and reproach yourselves, and call yourselves fools, and abhor yourselves, and smite upon your own breasts; nay, and if God give you grace, take a holy revenge upon yourselves (which is reckoned among the products of godly sorrow, 2 Cor. 7: 11);

and what can be more uneasy than all this? You take a
mighty liberty in chiding those that you have under your
power, and giving them very ill-favored language, because
you know they dare not chide you again; but dare not your
own hearts smite you, and your consciences chide you? And
is it not easier to bear the chidings of any man in the world
(which may either be avoided, or answered, or slighted),
than to bear the reproaches of our own consciences which, as
we cannot get out of the hearing of, so we cannot make a light
matter of? For when conscience is awake, it will be heard,
and will tell us home, wherein "we are verily guilty concerning our brother" (Gen. 42:21). Let this thought therefore quiet our spirits when they begin to be tumultuous, that
hereby we shall but make work for repentance; whereas, on
the contrary, as Abigail suggested to David, the bearing and
forgiving of an injury will be no trouble or grief of mind
afterwards. Let wisdom and grace therefore do that which
time will do: that is cool our heat, and take off the edge of
our resentment.

f. *That that is truly best for us* which is most pleasing
and acceptable to God, and that a meek and quiet spirit is
so. No principle has such a commanding influence upon the
soul as that which has a regard to God, and wherein we approve ourselves to him. It was a good hint which the woman
of Tekoah gave to David when she was suing for a merciful
sentence: "I pray thee, let the king remember the Lord thy
God" (2 Sam. 14: 11); nor could any thought be more ap-
peasing than that. Remember how gracious and merciful
and patient God is, how slow to anger, how ready to forgive, and how well pleased he is to see his people like him:
remember the eye of thy God upon thee, the love of thy
God towards thee, and the glory of thy God set before thee.
Remember how much it is thy concern to be accepted of
God, and to walk worthy of thy relation to him, unto all

well-pleasing; and how much meekness and quietness of
spirit does contribute to this, as it is consonant to that excellent religion which our Lord Jesus has established, and
as it renders the heart a fit habitation for the blessed Spirit.
"This is good and acceptable in the sight of God our Savior,
to lead quiet and peaceable lives" (1 Tim. 2:2, 3). It is a
good evidence of our reconciliation to God, if we be cor-
dially reconciled to every cross providence, which necessarily
includes a meek behavior toward those who are any ways
instrumental in the cross. Very excellently does St. Austin
express it: *Quis placet Deo? cui Deus placuerit* — "Those
please God who are pleased with him," and with all he
does, whether immediately by his own hand, or mediately
by the agency of provoking injurious men. This is standing
complete in all the will of God, not only his commanding
but his disposing will, saying, without reluctance, "The will
of the Lord be done." He that acts from an honest principle
of respect to God and sincerely desires to stand right in his
favor, cannot but be in some measure adorned with that
meek and quiet spirit, which he knows to be in the sight
of God of great price.

Such as these are softening principles, and as many as
walk according to these rules, peace shall be upon them, and
mercy, and no doubt it shall be upon the Israel of God.

V. *Some Rules of Direction*

The laws of our holy religion are so far from clashing and
interfering that one Christian duty does very much further
and promote another; the fruits of the Spirit are like links
in a chain, one draws on another; it is so in this; many
other graces contribute to the "ornament of a meek and
quiet spirit."

You see how desirable the attainment is. Will you therefore, through desire, *separate* yourselves to the pursuit of

it, and *seek* and "intermeddle with all wisdom?" (Prov.
18:1), and all little enough that you may reach to the
meekness of wisdom.

a. *Sit loose to the world and to everything in it.* The
more the world is crucified to us, the more our corrupt passions will be crucified *in* us. If we would keep calm and
quiet, we must by faith live above the stormy region. It
is certain that those who have anything to do in the world
cannot but meet with that every day from those with whom
they deal which will cross and provoke them; and if the
affections be set upon these things, and we be filled with a
prevailing concern about them, as the principal things,
those crosses must needs pierce to the quick, and inflame
the soul, and that which touches us in these things, touches
us in the apple of our eye. If the appetites be carried out
inordinately towards those things that are pleasing to sense,
the passions will be to the very same degree carried out
against those that are displeasing. And therefore Christians, whatever you have of the world in your hands, be it
more or less, as you value the peace as well as the purity
of your souls keep it out of your hearts, and evermore let
out your affections towards your possessions, enjoyments,
and delights in the world with a due consideration of the
disappointment and provocation which probably you will
meet with in them, and let that restrain and give check to
their inordinacy.

It is the excellent advice of Epictetus that we should consider the nature of the thing in which we take pleasure and
proportion our complacency accordingly: "If thou art in love
with a China cup, or a Venice glass, love it as a piece of brit-
tle ware, and then the breaking of it will be no great offence,"
nor put thee into any disturbing passion, for it is but what
thou didst expect. Those that idolize anything in this world
will be greatly discomposed if they be crossed in it. "The

money which Micah's mother had was her god, before it had the shape either of a graven or a molten image," says Bishop Hall, "else the loss of it would not have set her cursing as it did" (Judges 17:2). Those who are greedy of gain trouble their own hearts, as well as their own houses (Prov. 15: 27); they are a burden to themselves and a terror to all about them. They who will be rich, who are resolved upon it, come what will, cannot but fall into these foolish and hurtful lusts (1 Tim. 6:9). And those also who serve their own bellies, who are pleased with nothing unless it be wound up to the height of pleasure, who are like "the tender and delicate woman, that would not set so much as the sole of her foot to the ground for tenderness and delicacy," lie very open to that which is disquieting, and cannot without a great disturbance to themselves bear a disappointment; and therefore Plutarch, that great moralist, prescribes for the preservation of our *meekness* "not to be curious in diet, or clothes, or attendance; for they who need but few things, are not liable to anger if they be disappointed of many."

Would we but learn in these things to cross ourselves, we should not be so apt to take it unkind if another crosses us. And therefore the method of the lessons in Christ's school is first to "deny ourselves," and to "take up our cross" (Matt. 16:24). We must also mortify the desire of the applause of men as altogether impertinent to our true happiness. If we have learned not to value ourselves by their good word, we shall not much disturb ourselves for their ill word. St. Paul bore reproaches with much meekness because he did not build upon the opinion of men, reckoning it a small thing to be "judged of man's judgment" (1 Cor. 4: 3).

b. *Be often repenting of your sinful passion,* and renewing your covenants against it. If our rash anger were more bitter to us in the reflection afterwards, we should not be so apt to relapse into it. Repentance in general, if it be sound and deep, and grounded in true contrition and humiliation, is very meekening, and disposes the soul to bear injuries with abundance of patience. Those who live a life of repentance, as everyone of us has reason to do, cannot but live a quiet life; for nobody can lightly say worse of the true penitent than he says of himself. Call him a fool, an affront which many think deserves a challenge, and the humble soul can bear it patiently with this thought, "Yea, a fool I am," and I have called myself so many a time; "more brutish than any man, I have not the understanding of a man" (Prov. 30: 2). But repentance does in a special manner dispose us to meekness when it fastens upon any irregular inordinate passion with which we have been transported. Godly sorrow for our former transgressions in this matter will work a carefulness in us not to transgress again. If others be causelessly or excessively angry with me, am not I justly requited for the like or more indecent passions? Charge it home therefore with sorrow and shame upon your consciences, aggravating the sin, and laying a load upon yourselves for it, and you will find that "the burnt child," especially while the burn is smarting, "will dread the fire" (Job 42: 6).

With our repentance for our former unquietness, we must engage ourselves by a firm resolution in the strength of the grace of Jesus Christ to be more mild and gentle for the future. Say that "you will take heed to your ways that you offend not," as you have done, "with your tongue"; and be often remembering that you said so, as David does (Psalm 39: 1). Resolution would do much towards the conquering of the most rugged nature, and the quiet bearing of the greatest provocation; it would be like the bit and bridle to the horse and mule that have no understanding. It may be of good use every morning to renew a charge upon our affections to keep the peace, and having welcomed Christ in faith and meditation let no rude or unruly passion stir up or awake our love.

c. *Keep out of the way of provocation* and stand upon your guard against it. While we are so very apt to offend in this matter, we have need to pray, and to practice accordingly, "Lord, lead us not into temptation." Those are enemies to themselves and to their own peace, as well as to human society, who seek occasion of quarrel, who fish for provocations and dig up mischief; but meek and quiet people will on the contrary studiously avoid even that which is justly provoking, and will see it as if they saw it not. Those that would not be angry must wink at that which would stir up anger, or put a favorable construction upon it. The advice of the wise man is very good to the purpose, "Also take no heed to all the words that are spoken, lest thou hear thy servant curse thee" (Eccl. 7:21); and it is better for thee not to hear it, unless thou couldst hear it patiently, and not to be provoked to sin in the hearing of it. It is a common story of Cotys that being presented with a cupboard of curious glasses he returned his thanks to his friend who had sent them, and gratified the messenger who had brought them, and then deliberately broke them all lest by the casual breaking of them severally he should be provoked to passion. And Dion relates to the honor of Julius Caesar that Pompey's cabinet of letters coming to his hand, he would not read them because he was his enemy and he would be likely to find in them that which would increase the quarrel; and therefore, as Dr. Reynolds expresses it, "he chose rather to make a fire on his hearth than in his heart." *De non existentibus et non apparentibus eadem est ratio* — "Keep the injury out of sight, and it will be out of mind."

But seeing "briers and thorns are with us," and "we dwell among scorpions" (Ezek 2: 6), and it must needs be that offences will come, let us be so much the more careful, as we are when we go with a candle among barrels of gunpowder, and exercise ourselves to have consciences void of offence, not apt to offend others, nor to resent the offences of others. When we are at any time engaged in business or company where we foresee provocation, we must double our watch, and be more than ordinarily circumspect. "I will keep my mouth with a bridle," says David; that is, with a particular actual care and diligence, "while the wicked is before me," and frequent acts will confirm the good disposition and bring it to a habit. Plutarch advises this: "To set some time to ourselves for special strictness: so many days or weeks in which, whatever provocations do occur, we will not suffer ourselves to be disturbed by them." And thus he supposes, by degrees, the habit of vicious anger may be conquered and subdued. But after all, the grace of faith has the surest influence upon the establishment and quietness of the spirit. Faith established the mercy of God, the meekness of Christ, the love of the Spirit, the commands of the word, the promises of the covenant, and the peace and quietness of the upper world; this is the approved shield, with which we may be able "to quench all the fiery darts of the wicked one," and all his wicked instruments.

d. *Learn to pause.* It is a good rule, as in our communion with God, so in our converse with men to "Be not rash with thy mouth, and let not thine heart be hasty to utter any thing" (Eccl. 5: 2). When at any time we are provoked, delays may be as advantageous as in other cases they are dangerous. "The discretion of a man deferreth his anger" (Prov. 19: 11). Socrates said to his servant, *Caedissem nisi iratus essem* — "I would beat thee if I were not angry." He that is hasty of spirit, that joins in with his anger upon the first rise of it, "exalteth folly" (Prov. 14: 2, 9). The office of reason is to govern the passions, but then we must give time to act, and not suffer the tongue to overrun it. Some have advised when we are provoked to anger to take at least so much time to deliberate as it takes to repeat the alphabet; others have thought it more proper to repeat the Lord's Prayer, and perhaps by the time we are past the fifth petition — Forgive us our trespasses, as we forgive them that trespass against us — we may find our temper softened. "To think twice before we speak once" is a good rule, for "he that hasteth with his feet, sinneth." This was the noted saying of a great statesman in Queen Elizabeth's court: "Take time and we shall have done the sooner." Nor can there be anything lost by deferring our anger; for there is nothing said or done in our wrath, but it might be better said and better done in meekness.

e. *Pray to God by his Spirit to work in you* this excellent grace of meekness and quietness of spirit. It is a part of that comeliness which he puts upon the soul, and he must be sought unto for it. If any man lacks this meekness of wisdom, let him ask it of God, who gives liberally, and does not upbraid us with our folly. When we begin at any time to be froward and unquiet, we must lift a prayer to him who stills the noise of the sea, for that grace which establishes the heart. When David's heart was hot within him, the first word that broke out was a prayer (Psalm 39: 3, 4). When we are surprised with a provocation, and begin to be in a ferment upon it, it will not only be a present diversion, but a sovereign cure, to lift up an ejaculation to God for grace and strength to resist and overcome the temptation: "Lord, keep me quiet now!" In this matter "Let your requests be made known to God; and the peace of God shall keep your hearts and minds" (Phil. 4:6, 7). You are ready enough to complain of unquiet people about you; but you have more reason to complain of unquiet passion within you; the others are but thorns in the hedge, these are thorns in the flesh, against which, if you beseech the Lord, as Paul did (2 Cor. 12: 8), with faith, and fervency, and constancy, you shall receive "grace sufficient."

f. *Be often examining your growth and proficiency in this grace.* Inquire what ground you have got of your passion, and what improvements you have made in meekness. Provocations recur every day, such as have been wont perhaps to put you into a passion: these give you an opportunity to make the trial. Do you find that you are less subject to anger, and when angry that you are less transported by it than formerly? Do you find that your apprehension of injuries is less quick, and your resentments less keen than usual? Is the little kingdom of your mind more quiet than it has been, and the discontented party weakened and kept under? It is well if it be so, and a good sign that the soul prospers and "is in health." We should examine every night whether we have been quiet all day. We shall sleep the better if we can find that we have. Let conscience keep up a grand inquest in the soul, under a charge from the judge of heaven and earth to inquire and make due presentment of all riots, routs, and breaches of the peace. And let nothing be left unpresented for favor, affection, or self-love; nor let anything presented be left unprosecuted according to law. Those whose natural temper, or their age, or distemper, leads them to be hot, and hasty, and unquiet, have an opportunity by their meekness and gentleness to discover both the truth and strength of grace in general; for it is the surest mark of uprightness to keep ourselves "from our own iniquity" (Psalm 18:23). And yet, if the children of God bring forth these fruits of the Spirit in old age, when commonly men are most froward and peevish, it shows not only that they are upright, but rather that the Lord is upright, in whose strength they stand. It shows that he is their rock, and there "is no unrighteousness in him" (Psalm 42: 14, 15).

g. *Delight in the company of meek and quiet persons.* Solomon prescribes it as a preservative against foolish passion to "make no friendship with an angry man, lest thou learn his ways" (Prov. 22: 24, 25). When thy neighbor's heart is on fire it is time to look to thy own. But man is a sociable creature, and cut out for converse; let us, therefore, since we must have some company, choose to have fellowship with those who are meek and quiet that we may learn their way, for it is a good way. The wolf is no companion for the lamb, nor the leopard for the kid, till they have forgot to hurt and destroy. Company is assimilating, and we are apt insensibly to grow like those with whom we ordinarily converse, especially with whom we delight to converse; therefore, let the quiet in the land be the men of our choice, especially into standing relations and bosom-friendship. Observe in others how sweet and amiable meekness is, and what a heaven upon earth those enjoy who have the command of their own passions; and study to transcribe such copies. There are those who take a pleasure in riotous company, and are never well but when they are in the midst of noise and clamor. Heaven would not be heaven to such, for that is a calm and quiet region; no noise there, but what is sweet and harmonious.

h. *Study the cross of our Lord Jesus.* Did we but know more of Jesus Christ, and him crucified, we should experience more of the fellowship of his sufferings. Think often how and in what manner he suffered; see him led as a lamb to the slaughter, and arm yourselves with the same mind. Think also why and for what end he suffered so that you may not in anything contradict the design of your dying Savior, nor receive his grace in vain. Christ died as the great peace-maker, to take down all partition-walls, to quench all threatening flames, and to reconcile his followers, not only to God, but to one another by the "slaying of all enmities" (Eph. 2:14, 16). The apostle often prescribes a believing regard to the sufferings of Christ as a powerful allay to all sinful and intemperate heats (Eph. 10: 2 and Phil. 22:5). Those who would show forth the meek and humble life of Christ in their mortal bodies must "bear about with them continually the dying of the Lord Jesus" (2 Cor. 4:10). The ordinance of the Lord's supper in which we show forth the Lord's death, and the new testament in his blood, must therefore be improved by us for this blessed end, as a love-feast, at which all our sinful passions must be laid aside, and a marriage-feast, where the ornament of a meek, quiet spirit is a considerable part of the wedding-garment. The forgiving of injuries, and a reconciliation to our brother, is both a necessary branch of our preparation for that ordinance, and a good evidence and instance of our profiting by it. If God has there spoken peace to us, let us not go away and speak war to our brethren. The year of re-lease under the law, which put an end to all actions, suits, and quarrels, began in the close of the day of atonement; then the jubilee-trumpet sounded.

i. *Converse much in your thoughts with the dark and silent grave.* You meet with many things now that disturb and disquiet you, and much ado you have to bear them: think how quiet death will make you, and how incapable of resenting or resisting injuries; and what an easy prey this flesh of which you are so jealous will shortly be to the worm that shall feed sweetly on it. You will soon be out of the reach of provocation, there where the wicked cease from troubling, and where their envy and their hatred is forever perished. And is not a quiet spirit the best preparative for that quiet state? Think how all these things, which now disquiet us, will appear when we come to look death in the face: how small and inconsiderable they seem to one that is stepping into eternity. Think, "what need is there that I should so ill resent an affront or injury, that am but a worm today, and may be worms' meat tomorrow." They say when bees fight the throwing up of dust among them quickly parts the fray. A little sprinkling of the dust of the grave, which we are on the brink of, would do much towards the quieting of our spirits, and the taking up of our quarrels. Death will quiet us shortly; let grace quiet us now. When David's heart was "hot within him," he prayed, "Lord, make me to know my end" (Psalm 34: 3, 4).

In conclusion I wish to say that I know of no errand that I can come upon of this kind to you in which I should be more likely to prevail than in this: so much does meekness conduce to the comfort and repose of our own souls, and the making of our lives sweet and pleasant to us. "If thou be wise herein, thou shalt be wise for thyself." That which I have been so intent upon in this discourse, is only to persuade you not to be your own tormentors, but to govern your passions so that they may not be furies to yourselves. The ornament I have been recommending to you is confessedly excellent and lovely. Will you put it on, and wear it, that by this all men may know that you are disciples of Christ and that you may be found among the sheep, on the right hand, at the great day, when Christ's angels shall "gather out of his kingdom every thing that offends"? Every one will give meekness a good word; but in this, as in other instances, *Probitas laudatur et alget* — "Honesty is applauded, yet neglected."

Love is commended by all, and yet the love of many waxeth cold; but let all that would not be self-condemned practise what they praise. And as there is nothing in which it will easier appear whether I have prevailed or no; this tree will soon be known by its fruits; so many are the circumstances of almost every day which call for the exercise of this grace that our profiting therein will quickly appear to ourselves, and to all with whom we converse. Our meekness and quietness is more obvious, and falls more directly

under a trial and observation, than our love to God and our
faith in Christ, and other graces, the exercise whereof lies
more immediately between God and our own souls. Shall
we therefore set ourselves to manifest, in all our converse,
that we have indeed received good by this plain discourse;
that our relations and neighbors, and all with whom we have
dealings, may observe a change in us for the better, and
may take knowledge of us that we have been with Jesus?
And let not the impressions of it ever wear off, but living
and dying, let us be found among the "quiet in the land."
We all wish to see quiet families, and quiet churches, and
quiet neighborhoods, and quiet nations; and it will be so
if there be quiet hearts; and not otherwise.

Made in the USA
Columbia, SC
14 September 2020